Robert Sowers

THE LANGUAGE OF STAINED GLASS

ROBERT SOWERS

The Language of Stained Glass

Published by Timber Press, Forest Grove, Oregon

THE LANGUAGE OF STAINED GLASS

Robert Sowers

ISBN 0-917304-61-6

© Copyright 1981 by Robert Sowers

LIBRARY OF CONGRESS CATALOGING
IN PUBLICATION DATA

Sowers, Robert
  The language of stained glass.
  Includes bibliographical references.
  1. Glass painting and staining—History I. Title.
NK5306.S68   748.59   80-29703
ISBN 0-917304-61-6

PRINTED IN THE UNITED STATES OF AMERICA

For Terry

CONTENTS

INTRODUCTION

Although this book grows out of and in a few places leans rather heavily upon an earlier one, *Stained Glass: An Architectural Art,* it is essentially a new book with a distinct concern of its own. To begin with, the subject is a great deal richer than one could have imagined fifteen years ago, if only because of the unprecedented revival of stained glass in Germany which was then just coming into its own. But it also presents the would-be interpreter with a far more complex challenge than I realized when that book was published. Then it seemed sufficient to define the crucial if little-understood relation between stained glass and architecture; now I am far more aware of how necessary it is to distinguish the aims and resources of this art from those of easel painting. Then it seemed sufficient, in a final chapter, to dissect some of the most debilitating misconceptions about religious art with which the stained-glass artist had long had to contend; this time it seemed far more important to question some of the equally burdensome parochialisms of the contemporary art world. Withal, the object of this book is still the same: to show what, on the evidence of its history, is central and what is peripheral to stained glass as an art form in its own right.

In such an inquiry nothing is more instructive than the casual assumptions of otherwise thoughtful and perceptive critics, in which the basic misconceptions about one's subject are most plausibly, persuasively — and authoritatively — enshrined. It is precisely there that error must be called into account. Hence this book is inescapably polemical; but because it is concerned with fundamentals it not only shirks no difficulties, it seeks them out. Confronted with some persistent misconception, there is no better way to disarm it than to recognize everything that can be said in its *favor* and still show where it goes wrong. Our subject demands no less. Because the matters with which the book is concerned are primarily visual I have not hesitated on occasion to go rather far afield for an example that graphically illustrated some point, especially in the chapters on light. This is not a mere photo-journalistic device, for as we shall see, the language of stained glass derives far more of its essential qualities from light and the light-adaptive behavior of human vision than it does from the the color-saturated expressionistic painting with which it is so commonly yet superficially associated. Basking in the aura of a color-emblazoned window, the viewer is ill-equipped to realize that it is the luminosity, the vibrancy, the almost respiratory value inflections of the glass rather than the color itself to which he is largely responding; yet such is the case. For ultimately, color in stained glass is dispensable while these other qualities,

Left: 1. Medallion window, north choir aisle, Canterbury Cathedral, early 13th century; detail.

which are so immediately and finally compelling, are not. Its most singular effects, its vital import, its primary rationale as an art form, all derive in the last analysis from the cultivated play of natural light.

Hence the somewhat extended discussion of light with which this book begins. Far from being the digression it may seem at first thought to be, it is really the key to everything else that follows. In dealing with matters of art there is a tendency, at least as old as the Romans, to reduce all of the dynamic, relational elements to the most static, piecemeal formulae. As P.A. Michelis reminds us, the original Greek word for an architectural order was *rhythmos,* or rhythm — an infinitely more vital, subtle and perceptually astute conception than is contained in the term "order." *Ordo* was "adopted by the Romans, who saw in Greek styles only the external arrangement of the architectural members."[1] If this tendency were no more than the dead hand of academicism that would be sufficient grounds for condemning it; but in the case of an art form like stained glass it becomes truly intolerable, hampering the discussion at every turn. Once the dynamic, relational qualities of light are understood, however — physically, psychologically and aesthetically — the function of all the elements that variously contribute to the appearance of a stained-glass window, from architecture to glasspainting, become apparent and fall into place. Whatever their particular merits *as* architecture or *as* painting, they can be seen for what they are as elements in *this* art: so many distinctive ways of modulating light. To the inveterate Roman amongst my readers, who nevertheless cannot rest content until he learns how the glass is colored or cut or whatever, I can only say: Begin with Chapter VII; but the book, like the subject itself, begins and ends with light.

For this reason I have employed colorplates only where color is essential to the matters under discussion. Elsewhere, its absence may be taken not merely as evidence of economic austerity but as a positive demonstration of my thesis that, second only to light, the other most distinctive and indispensable quality in the language of stained glass glass is *graphic structure.* Graphic structure and light. These are the qualities that unite the two styles, otherwise so different, that I consider to be most instructive: that of the 12th and early 13th centuries and that of present-day Germany — the one ancient and indelible in its effect upon almost everyone, the other still very much alive yet only now beginning to receive the general recognition it deserves.

It remains only to make clear what I have not attempted to do in the pages that follow. As concerned as I am to make sense of the history of stained glass — to account for its mercurial rise, subsequent decline and present revival at least in broad outline — this book is neither a survey nor a historical study in the strict sense. No attributions are challenged, dates disputed or esoteric symbols deciphered. Nor does it logroll for any of the latest interactions between stained glass and Pop, Minimal or Conceptual art, or attempt to show everything that is being done, even by the leading German stained-glass artists. In what purports to be a fundamental reinterpretation of so notoriously misunderstood an art form the very latest work is only occasionally likely to be the most instructive. Rather, I have chosen to illustrate it with works that

Left: 2. Ludwig Schaffrath: *Emperor* window, Church of Sts. Peter and Paul, Heilbronn, 1969; detail.

first of all are good of their kind, relevant to the text, complementary to one another, and competently photographed. My reasons for doing so will become apparent to the reader in Chapter XI. And finally, the book does not go into technical matters any further than necessary or flaunt the jargon of the craft where plain English will do; it is about the *art*.

In addition to *Stained Glass: An Architectural Art,* New York, 1965, I have drawn upon the following previously published materials: "On the Blues in Chartres," *Art Bulletin,* XLVIII, 1966; "The 12th-Century Windows in Chartres: Some Wayward Lessons from the 'Poor Man's Bible'," *Art Journal,* XVII, Winter 1968-69; and "New Stained Glass in Germany," *Craft Horizons,* XXIX, May-June 1969. I am indebted to the studios of Dr. H. Oidtmann and Derix/Rottweil for much valuable assistance; to Rowan LeCompte and the Walters Gallery for the opportunity to photograph the *Thadeus* panel during the course of its restoration; to the many artists who generously supplied photographs; to Nat LaMar for his expert critical assistance; and most of all to Judi Jordan for breathing life back into this book after a tragic hiatus.

New York City, May 1980   R.S.

PART ONE: PAINTING WITH LIGHT

Observe the play of shadows, learn the game ... Precise shadows, clear cut or dissolving. Projected shadows, sharp. Projected shadows, precisely delineated, but what enchanting arabesques and frets. Counterpoint and fugue. Great music.

— Le Corbusier

I Discovering What Was "Lost"

Even today we hardly understand the language of the stained-glass window.
— André Malraux

Since time immemorial the revealing energy of light has stood as an almost irresistible image or analogue for clarity, vitality and by extension all that is good; its absence for obscurity, stasis and evil. But from this phenomenon, which has captivated mankind throughout the ages and inspired some of the greatest art, our mechanically oriented civilization has abstracted a kind of static functional illumination (not unlike the bland "daylight" effects of engineers) to which it attaches a privileged Reality. So ingrained is this mode of seeing that we tend to study the arts in a luminous vacuum, as if the play of light on architecture, sculpture, stained glass and mosaic were merely accidental.[1] Or where that effect is so impressive that it cannot be wholly ignored, as in the Pantheon or the cathedral of Chartres, we tend either to treat it as a sublime curiosity or, lapsing into a state of credulous self-bedazzlement, attribute it to almost anything — anything that is sufficiently incomprehensible. Thus two apparently different realms of expressive phenomena — the impersonal but deeply affective powers of light and the most exalted creations of man, each indisputably visible, compelling, and in its own distinctive way capable of stirring our deepest feelings — compete unnaturally and inconclusively for our attention.

Nowhere are the consequences of this perceptual conflict more graphically evident than in the still prevalent tendency to think of stained glass as "little more than" a strangely intractible mode of painting. Here is an art form, after all, that in many respects could hardly be more alien to the art of painting as it has generally been understood for the past five hundred years. To begin with, its sheer physical attraction is such that even the simplest bona fide creation, like the Matisse windows in Vence, refuses to be *mere* decoration. It is an art form in which the most seemingly incongruous elements — pure design, mechanically necessary structure, and plain visual accident — are fused in such a beguiling dialectic that each in its turn may appear to be the dominant factor in creating some particular effect. A leadline that is an obvious mechanical necessity at one point becomes pure drawing at another and calls attention to its unadulterated material quiddity at still another. The most carefully established color relations are endlessly enhanced here and prejudiced there by a mad chiaroscuro of local variations in the value and intensity of the individual colors, caused by variations in the thickness of the glass. The whole window or ensemble of windows is constantly subject to the even more radical transformations — some dazzling and others all but nullifying — that result from changes in the balance of the light. So completely is the stained-glass window a creature of the light in which it is seen that even the windows in Chartres, emblazoned with the most vibrant palette of colors to be found anywhere in the arts, seem strangely apparitional — like some vast chorus of aeolian harps attuned to the whims of the sun and sky. And yet as we shall see, that attunement, seemingly so artless and unwilled, is every bit as rational and controlled as the perfect exposure of a photographic film.

Or consider: the greatest cathedral windows not only predate the emergence of painting as the dominant art; they predate by more than half a century every technical advance in their own craft that, later on, would increase its painterly facility. To be sure, they contain some beautiful calligraphic *drawing* — probably the most beautiful brush drawing in all of Western art — but to single out this one element for almost exclusive attention is not only to do violence to the medieval aesthetic; it is to distract attention from precisely those qualities that, taken together and grasped in the logic and splendor of their interrelation, constitute the special glory of those works. In fact, there is nothing in this brush drawing that would enable us to account for the manner in which the cathedral windows reveal a whole panoply of effects *sequentially,* in obedience to the dicatates of the sun and clouds; nothing that even remotely helps us to account for the immediacy and pervasiveness of their aura. In these respects the glass in Chartres actually seems closer to music than to painting. The leadline, the elemental bond between delineated form and physical structure in 12th- and 13th-century stained glass, is from the point of view of painting little more than a wearisome confinement; the intrinsic richness of early glass as a material little more than an intriguing distraction. And the authority that the cathedral windows derive from being significantly more luminous than anything else in their surroundings is, when approached from the point of view of painting, a complete terra incognita. Thus by intellectual default the seeming "miracle" of the ancient windows remains almost exactly what it was to the Gothic Revivalists of a century ago, and for detractors and admirers alike the art of stained glass remains couched in an aura of inscrutability. We find Bernard Berenson in his later years still wondering "how much art, as distinct from mere craft, there is in our best twelfth- and thirteenth-century stained-glass windows," a question which he proceeded to answer with magnificent irrelevance in his most irritating bad-boy manner: "Their pattern is not easy to decipher, so much is it melted into the colour; and when deciphered how inferior it is in appeal! I have seen windows, not mere fragments, but entire windows, from St. Denis removed from the interior they were intended to transfigure, and I confess that one's enjoyment of them thus isolated was not so different from the Rajah's gloating over handfuls of emeralds, rubies and other precious stones."[2] *Thus isolated*; in a restorer's workshop presumably, and seen under who knows what light conditions. With equal authority he might have speculated upon the effect of the early morning sunlight through the *Mona Lisa.* For André Malraux, by contrast, the stained-glass windows in

Chartres were "the supreme paintings of the West, before Giotto," even though the language of stained glass remained a confessed mystery: it had not yet been "rescued from the medley of strapwork in which Our Lady of the Great Window is engulfed."[3]

As the history of stained glass-as-painting progresses, however, it runs into an even greater difficulty. For it is a demonstrable fact that at *some* point, which not even the most sanguine interpreter can postpone forever, the influence of painting upon stained glass began to turn into a distinct liability. Beyond that point there can be no question that the more zealously artists sought to make painting alone "carry" the stained-glass window the more blatantly obtrusive its structural fabric of leadlines and mullions became. The more convincingly they managed to depict their subjects in a fullblown three-dimensional world of their own the more such imaginary spaces tended to clash with the real architectural spaces in which their windows were set. And the more they sought to reproduce the effects of light and shade the more haphazard became the attunement of their windows to the actual luminous environment in which, willy nilly, they were destined to be viewed, so that some later windows appear strident and glaring while others are almost suffocatingly muted in their overall effect. Because the history of stained glass-as-painting cannot possibly account for this conflict between the two arts it defaults a second time — but historians go on studying, appraising, and as we shall later see, even visually documenting stained glass as though it were essentially an art of painting. So conceived, the history of stained glass becomes a kind of success story in self-immolation, a story that ends ignominiously in the 18th century with a "lost art" whose loss is never satisfactorily accounted for, and whose subsequent revival is generally ignored altogether.

Even more intellectually embarrassing than these conceptual difficulties, however, serious as they are, is the attempt by some writers to explain them *away.* Thus one critic, John Canaday, seeking to isolate Renaissance stained glass from any possible comparison with that of the Middle Ages, would have us believe that it is a different art form altogether.[4] Which one is "really" stained glass and what the other one is he does not bother to tell us — nor what is left of the usual distinction between medium and style. And an art historian, James Johnson, argues that Renaissance windows "were perfectly in accord with certain religious and aesthetic requirements of their time."[5] Perfectly; yet surely it requires no Gothic bias to wonder whether the conflict between image and leadline that by the mid-16th century had become almost endemic was ever perfectly in accord with anything.

Obviously, to anticipate some of the arguments of this book, painting is an element *in* stained glass, sometimes more and sometimes less important, but not its raison d'etre *as* an art form. To be sure, the stained-glass artist is just as concerned with line, form, tone, color and texture as any painter; but these after all are the common property of all the visual arts. What is not only unique but absolutely indispensable to stained glass is, to say it again, its graphic structure and its relation to light. And the "lost art" is, far more than anything else, a lost feeling for the logic of the one and the dynamics of the other.

But how, it may be asked, could such a loss have come about? Here one can only speculate, for we are talking about a complex shift in visual orientation that took place only gradually over the course of centuries. Prior to the advent of illusionistic art the formal, structural and expressive qualities of the various arts were, if not always exploited, never systematically suppressed in the interest of anything else. While there was no consistent "truth to materials" no one art loomed as the unchallenged model to be emulated by all of the others. But with the conquest of natural appearances this situation changed. All of the arts began to aspire to the quality that painting seemed most nearly to possess: a total plasticity, untrammeled by the dictates or inherent formal qualities of any material or technique. For a truly illusionistic art requires that the artist's medium become as nearly as possible the invisible servant of that illusion. This was a requirement that all of the arts resisted to some extent, but it was a requirement that stained glass could not possibly meet. Pursued to the bitter end despite every conceivable technical difficulty it could only be what in fact it was: the kiss of death, a chilling triumph of aesthetic doctrine over sensibility.

To recognize it as such, as I think we must, entails no wholesale condemnation of Renaissance art such as occurred in the 19th century, and to which Canaday's and Johnson's arguments are such a belated reaction. It is fully compatible with the realization that in those arts where the imagination could exercise its newly won sovereignty without doing any such violence to the medium — in architecture, in sculpture, in wall painting — the Renaissance provided a new impetus that lasted until, roughly, the death of Tiepolo. Nor does it entail any special allegiance to medieval art. After all, the most that the Middle Ages could do for the stained-glass artist of the 19th century was to instruct him in the long-neglected fundamentals of his craft; once these had been rediscovered, the medieval style in which they were clothed proved to be a far more tenacious obstacle to creation than any ill-fitting classicism. What it obviously does entail perhaps more than anything else is a new receptivity to the behavior of light; indeed, the art of stained glass recalls us to an aesthetics of light that, as Kim Levin has shown, is at least as old as the temple architecture of the early Egyptian dynasties.[6] And this is a subject to which the painting-dominated conception of art can bring nothing but a kind of patronizing confusion;[7] we are forced to begin anew.

II *The Signal Ambience*

Light is a physical force whose source, direction, intensity and impact on the world around us are all visibly and affectively evident. The singular richness of natural light, with which we shall be primarily concerned, is due first of all to the fact that it is a combination of focused and diffused light. The sun, which is ninety-three million miles from the earth, functions as a point source of light; but its effect is always qualified to a greater or lesser degree by the earth's atmospheric envelope through which it must pass, and which also functions like a vast secondary source of diffused light itself. In order to realize how essential this combination of direct *and* diffused light is to our sense of wellbeing one need only to recall the eery effects of the photographs taken on the moon, where the intense glare of the sun is unrelieved by any atmospheric illumination of the sky; or the deadening effect of a heavy overcast day when the whole world seems to be enshrouded in a pervasive gloom. To describe the elementary properties of natural light is therefore to note first of all how the appearance of the sun is modified by the elements.

On a clear day the location and therefore the movement of the sun across the sky is readily apparent and, to the observant eye, perceptibly orderly, as are the accompanying changes in the color and intensity of the light. Whatever one's knowledge of astronomy or lack of it, the rhythmic alternation of day and night contains us all, orders our existence like a kind of cosmic metronome. But clear skies alternate with more or less cloudy ones in a sequence that is not at all orderly, or at least not perceptibly so from one hour to the next, and the regular waxing and waning of light is often dramatically altered in its character and intensity by the apparent vicissitudes of changing atmospheric conditions. Thus clarity and obscurity, order and randomness constantly vie with one another with an evocative power that has no rival in nature or art.

So much for the intrinsic properties of natural light itself. Equally important is the way light defines form and form in its turn defines light. This can best be understood by ignoring for the moment one highly important phenomenon: the different reflecting powers of various materials which determines both their color and their particular dark-and-light value or tonality. Assuming then a colorless world of objects of uniform value illuminated by a diffuse light — a world not unlike that sometimes evoked in black-and-white photographs of monochromatic subjects — in such a world the light, which seems to come from everywhere and nowhere, appears almost to be an intrinsic property of the subjects themselves. Our principal cues to the three-dimensional substance of things in such a world are the softly modulated shadows of forms as they

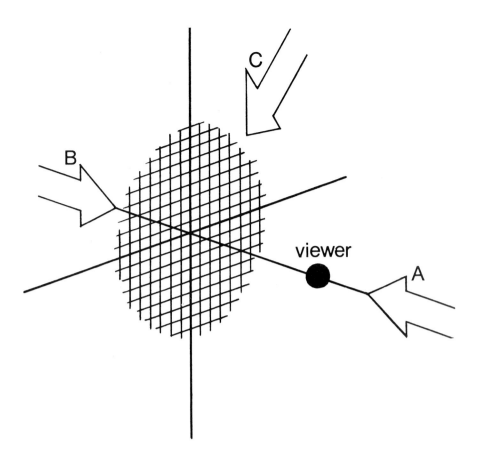

turn away from the plane perpendicular to the viewer, or appear to be farther from the source of light.

To the degree that the light becomes focused rather than diffused, shadows will acquire contours and, depending upon the location of the light source in relation to both the viewer and the things illuminated, they will take on certain distinctive qualities. Generally speaking, the nearer the light source is to the viewer's line of sight, as represented by the line AB in our diagram, the *less* informative it will be, whether it is directly behind him (A) or directly behind his subject (B). In the first case, shadows become all but invisible and the subject will take on a kind of hard cameo-like flatness; in the second case, the subject, silhouetted against the light will become almost entirely obscured by shadow, and the viewer may even have to contend with the light source itself shining directly into his eyes. Both extremes, however, have long fascinated painters and photographers precisely because of their limitations. Radically different from either is the effect of what photographers call "raking" light — light which comes from a position that is more or less at right angles to the viewer's line of sight (C), whether to one side or overhead, and which seems quite literally to rake across the surfaces of his subjects, throwing their every deviation from flatness into the boldest possible relief. To the degree that light comes from some intermediate position between these two principal axes it will relinquish some of the qualities of the first and take on those of the second, but its most characteristic effects will be of a different order. Shad-

3. Light sources (A, B or C) in relation to subject (grid) and viewer.

ows will tend to echo, ornament, parody or reinforce the contours of subjects or envelop them in a world of darkness; or occasionally they may even take on a positive role as subjects of intrinsic interest themselves. If shadows are considered projections of darkness into the world of light, reflections may be seen as the counterprojection of light into shadow. As such they can be seen to take on some of the same functions as shadows.

Into our hypothetical world of uniform grayness we may now introduce the three additional variables which in combination with those already described largely determine the impact of daylight upon our natural environment: translucency, transparency and refraction. That the terms translucency and transparency are often used rather loosely as synonyms is testimony to a widespread confusion about the the difference between these two qualities, a difference that it will be important for us to keep in mind. Trans*luc*ency, as its Latin root indicates, means simply having the capacity to transmit light; trans*par*ency, as its root indicates, means having the capacity to transmit appearances as well. Generally, we do not perceive that any material object or surface is translucent except when the light that strikes it from the far side (B in our diagram) is more intense than that which strikes it from the viewer's side; and the more dense the material in question, the greater the difference between these two light levels must be. By the same token, the greater the difference actually happens to be in any given instance the more translucent a particular substance will appear to be. Thus the soft warm glow of the alabaster windows in the 6th-century tomb of Galla Placidia is a direct product of the extreme difference between the basic light levels inside and outside that building; when viewed under more typical light conditions alabaster appears almost as opaque as any other fine stone. In fact, there is no hard and fast division between the apparent translucency and opacity of *any* given material, even colored glass, except under a specified light condition. Nor is there any such division between the qualities of translucency and transparency; the atmosphere is noticeably more transparent when the humidity is low than when there is a great amount of moisture in the air.

But with transparency we become aware of *refraction,* or the degree to which the appearance of things is distorted by the medium or substance through which they are seen. Such distortions can be due to either of two factors, the density or the surface irregularity of the substance through which the light must pass. Thus light waves passing from the air into water are slowed down by the greater density of the latter, with the familiar result that the straight shaft of an oar will appear to be bent where it enters the water. And as the surface of the water undulates the second distortion can be seen: the immersed part of the oar will appear to be undulating as well. If we think of glass as a liquid that "freezes" at a high temperature we can better understand the various refractory qualities that are blown or pressed into it while it is in a molten state — a subject to which we shall return in Chapter VI.

Thus far we have been concerned to show how shadows, reflections and the translucency of certain materials acting separately or in combination would define the apperance of things in a hypothetically colorless world. But no de-

Left: 4. Fire-escape shadows in the cast-iron district, New York.

scription of this process would be complete that did not take into account the manner in which the appearance of these phenomena themselves is affected by the *scale* at which they are perceived to function — scale in relation to the total visual field of the observer. Where shadows or reflections occur on a scale sufficient to envelop the viewer and thus become the visual base against which he must measure everything else, as sometimes happens in the streets of lower Manhatttan, their impact can be literally environmental. At this scale the shadow cast by one building upon another may even be commanding enough to assume figurative characteristics in its own right. Or it may become the perfect foil for an ethereal grid of reflections from some neighboring building. As the sun changes its position not only from hour to hour but from one season to another the permutations upon these patterns seem endless. Where shadows are generally more linear than massive, as are the shadows of tree limbs or certain industrial apparatus, they will tend to impose a more or less regular grid of light and shade upon some part of our environment — sometimes a quite substantial part of it. And no matter how transient the light conditions may be which create such effects, or how much our pragmatically oriented vision tries to screen them out of consciousness, their capacity to enliven the appearance of otherwise plain surfaces or even to become major compositional elements in photographs is indisputable.

Where the scale of shadows is sufficiently reduced and their interaction becomes sufficiently repetitious, as for example on the masonry of a wall or even the foilage of a plant, the play of light and shade will tend to take on definite pattern characteristics. When this process of fragmentation is carried still further, to the point where our ability to perceive the play of individual units of light and shade is outweighed by our awareness of their overall homogeneity, pattern will give way to texture. And finally, where the fragmentation of light takes place on so small a scale as to be below the threshold of visual discrimination it can still have a very perceptible effect upon the surface appearance of things. In order to appreciate this one need only to compare the appearance of a piece of cabinetwork before and after it has received its final finish. Before the pores of the wood are sealed and its surface fibers smoothed down the depth and richness of its color will be largeiy obscured by the microscopic diffusion of light caused by these surface irregularities. It is only when that surface is in effect "glazed" by two or three layers of carefully buffed finish that the full depth of its color and the pattern of its grain become apparent.

With the introduction of color and thus of intrinsic material lightness and darkness into our hypothetical world it begins to resemble the world in which we live, not only in its richness but in the ambiguity for which this last quality is responsible. For the eye, which is sensitive only to patterns of varying light intensity, has no immmediate way of distinguishing between the appearance of a dimly illuminated light-colored object and one that is dark-colored but brightly illuminated if both happen to reflect the same amount of light upon the retina; it can do so only contextually. Thus, as painters and stage designers long ago discovered, the eye can be effectively deceived where the normal depth cues of light and shade are systematically manipulated. Suffice it to

Left: 5. Environmental shadows and reflections, lower Manhattan.

say that when the viewer has no clear comprehension of how shadows, reflections and translucency normally function to define the appearance of things he is all the more likely to be confused by the additional factor of color or tonality. But by now the point of this digression into the subject of pure light phenomena ought to be clear: however complex, evanescent, or elusive the effects of light may be, *their behavior is always orderly, and because it is orderly it can be consciously exploited by artists and architects.* Indeed, for tens of centuries it apparently was so exploited almost as routinely and matter-of-factly as sailors exploited the forces of winds and tides. *In*sensitivity to such order is probably, from a long-term historical point of view, far more an aberration than the rule; mere bedazzlement by the effects of light less a celebration of the sublime than a confession of our own present-day visual illiteracy.

To the art of stained glass the ideal viewer would bring the kind of sensibility, at once leisurely, measured and practical, that is evident in the following passage from John Ruskin, on the problem of drawing leaves: "Nearly all leaves have some lustre, and all are more or less translucent (letting light through them): therefore, in any given leaf, besides the intricacies of its own proper shadows and foreshortenings, there are three series of circumstances which alter or hide its forms. First, shadows cast on it by other leaves, — often very forcibly. Secondly, light reflected from its lustrous surface, sometimes the blue of the sky, sometimes the white of clouds, or the sun itself flashing like a star. Thirdly, forms and shadows of other leaves, seen as darknesses through the translucent parts of the leaf; a most important element of foliage effect, but wholly neglected by landscape artists in general.

"The consequence of all this is, that except now and then by chance, the form of a complete leaf is never seen; but a marvelous and quaint confusion, very definite, indeed, in its evidence of direction and growth, and unity of action, but wholly indefinable and inextricable, part by part, by any amount of patience. You cannot possibly work it out in facsimile, though you took a twelvemonth's time to a tree; and you must therefore try to discover some mode of execution which will more or less imitate, by its own variety and mystery, the variety and mystery of Nature, without absolute delineation of detail."[1]

Left: 6. "A marvelous and quaint confusion . . ."

III *Inside Light vs. Outside Light*

Everything that has been said up to this point has been said as it were against the luminous backdrop of the sky functioning as the unchallenged determinant of visual appearances. But in fact, the appearance of natural light is always itself subject to modification, even radical modification, depending upon the circumstances under which it is seen. Consider, for example, the experience of a driver passing through a tunnel on a clear sunny day. As he enters the tunnel his eyes are forced to adapt themselves to a range of light values that is perhaps less than one-tenth of that outside. In a remarkably short time they do so; the initial gloom of the tunnel is largely dispelled. Then shortly he begins to become aware of the intense glare at the further end of the tunnel. Once again his eyes are forced to make a radical adjustment, which they do so spontaneously and efficiently that in almost no time at all the outside world has resumed its normal appearance. Because our eyes are constantly being called upon to make light adaptations of this kind it is only under rather extreme circumstances that we become more than marginally aware of the process at all, and yet it is absolutely fundamental to any understanding of how natural light actually appears to us. Since it is the basic yardstick against which all other light values are ultimately measured, not only physically but psychologically, we tend to regard the appearance of natural light as though it were somehow immutable — at all times the product of remote physical and meteorological forces that are utterly beyond our control. But as our example makes clear, this is true only up to a point; ultimately the apparent brightness of daylight is always subject to modification — even extreme modification — by the conditions under which it is seen.

It follows that the creator of any interior space not only can but absolutely will affect to some degree the apparent brightness of any daylight that is visible through its windows: *the darker the space the greater that modification will be.* In the cathedral of Chartres, for example, the basic light level is so low that it takes several minutes for the eyes to adapt to it fully,[1] and as we shall later see, it is to this more than anything else that the singular radiance of its windows is due. But first we must consider the other ways in which the appearance of daylight is affected by being brought indoors.

Except at dawn or sunset, or under some other unusual circumstances, we tend to perceive exterior daylight as an all-enveloping luminous backdrop for our activities. But to create an interior space is not only to exclude a considerable part of that light but to channel the rest. A window is almost by definition a distinct light *source* with a fixed orientation to the sun and to the walls,

7. Rembrandt: *A Scholar Studying,* 1631, National Museum, Stockholm.

ceiling and other elements of an architectural space. As a result of being channeled through such a discrete opening daylight becomes to a greater or lesser
degree focused, or specifically directional; hence it will tend to create distinct
shadows, far more defined and substantial than those created by a full hazy
sky but of course far less sharp and contrasty than those created by direct
sunlight. As a further result of being so channeled the light from a window
will tend to produce an aura that visibly decreases in intensity the further
it penetrates into some otherwise unilluminated space, thus creating the infinite
gradations of half-light that were so hauntingly painted by Rembrandt. So
prevalent are these qualities — the apparent intensification of visible exterior

STONEHENGE

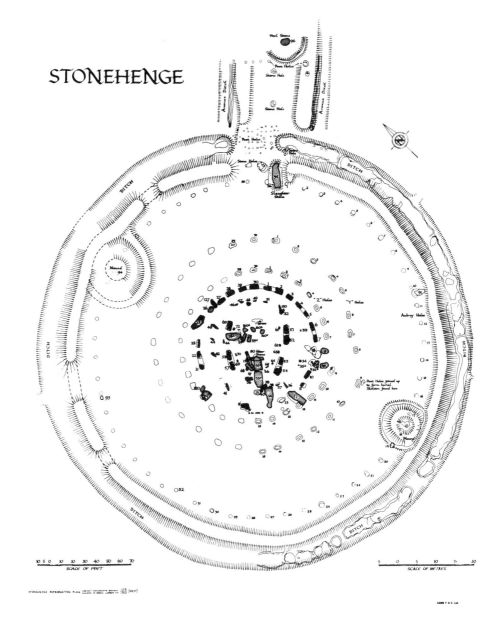

light, the semi-focused shadows, and the graduated diminutions of light —
that they may almost be said to determine the appearance of the interior
luminous environment where it is not also pierced by the direct rays of the
sun or artificially illuminated. A brief examination of four ancient structures
will enable us to see how masterfully these qualities of interior light have been
exploited, almost since the dawn of civilization.

Although Stonehenge is only marginally an interior space since it is and presumably always was open to the sky, it enables us for that very reason to
observe the powerful effect that may sometimes result primarily from the orientation of a structure to the sun. As is well known, Stonehenge is laid out
so that on midsummer's day the sun rises directly behind the "heel stone,"
thus casting its first rays along the central axis of the monument. The effect
is out of all proportion to the actual physical scale or venerability of this
neolithic stone circle. It is an effect that remains undiminished even when
scholars conclude, as they recently have, that the solar and lunar alignments

8. Stonehenge, site plan.

Right: 9. Stonehenge, sunrise on Midsummer's Day.

of Stonehenge were never precise enough for it to have functioned "as an accurate observatory."[2] For we are reckoning here not with the mathematical tolerances of modern astronomy but with a far more elemental visual phenomenon. Just as the monument is physically aligned with the sun, so the sun appears to be visually aligned with *it*, in a compelling one-to-one relationship that has captivated mankind for nearly four thousand years.

Compared to Stonehenge the Pantheon is almost monolithically enclosed, its boldly coffered dome saved from outright oppressiveness only by the large central oculus which is directly open to the sky. The dome is in fact a perfect hemisphere set upon a cylindrical wall of the same height, so that the interior of the building actually contains a completely spherical space. Thus the viewer entering the Pantheon finds himself within a realm of absolute symmetry that is at all times permeated with an evenly diffused light. However, the oculus of the Pantheon is open not only to the sky but to the direct rays of the sun as well, and this converts what might otherwise have been no more than a very imposing symbol of Roman authority into a far more compelling and universal image. For the direct rays of the sun, entering the Pantheon as a shaft of pure radiant light energy, never on axis, constantly in motion, seem to confer the transient bloom of a heightened reality upon whatever they chance to strike. Thus does this extraordinary monument seem almost to comment upon its own pretensions, to reveal in the most tangible way its subjection to a higher order that, although equally palpable — for the Pantheon is still Pagan to the core — is infinitely more powerful, more complex, more remote from human affairs.

The Pantheon was created c. 120 A.D. Two hundred years later the expansive, sceptical, material ethos of the Romans was giving way to a radically

10. The Pantheon, Rome, c. 120 A.D., sectional elevation.

Right: 11. Off-axial sunlight in the dome of the Pantheon.

12. S. Costanza, Rome, c. 350 A.D.

Right: 13. St-Philibert Abbey, Tournus, early 11th century.

different world view, as may be seen in the Church of S. Costanza. Like the Pantheon under whose influence it was undoubtedly built, S. Costanza is a centrally planned structure with its dome the principal source of light; but there the resemblance between the two buildings ends. Whereas the light playing upon the massive coffers of the vaulting of the Pantheon creates an almost overwhelming sense of materiality, that striking the unarticulated surfaces of the later structure seems almost completely self-effacing by comparison. And whereas the interior of the Pantheon is at all times pervaded with an even light, here the light is noticeably dissipated before it reaches the peripheral aisles, whose vaults are effectively veiled in deep shadow. Thus S. Costanza, for all of its residual classicism, has already begun to evoke the delineaments of a radically different, otherworldly realm into which the direct rays of the sun can enter as no more than a remote and fragmentary intrusion.

To trace the further unfolding of this new development, first of all in Ravenna and then the Byzantine world, would be to stray far beyond the requirements of our subject. Suffice it to say that by the 6th century the twilight atmosphere that is already implicit in S. Costanza had become the norm, and windows little more than a constellation of quasi-point light sources. But in the process they had begun to acquire the singular radiance evident, for example, in the west windows of Tournus Abbey. At once brilliant yet strangely remote, their light seems curiously self-contained — almost as if it had been arrested at the physical plane of the windows themselves, where it seems to hover in its shadowy surroundings like some insistent wraithlike presence. Thus was born, however inadvertently, the light of the earliest stained-glass windows.

IV *Metamorphosis of the Window*

Of the elements of a room the window is the most marvelous. The great American poet, Wallace Stevens, prodded the architect, "What slice of the sun does your building have?"

— Louis Kahn

The earliest *glazed* windows of the 6th, 7th and 8th centuries, however crude they may have been, must already have been stained-glass windows of a sort. That is to say, they must have been composed of many small pieces of glass assembled in some kind of latticework, since no one piece of early glass would ever have been large enough to fill even a comparatively small window opening; and the glass in them must have been at least tinted if not fully colored, since the technique of producing a clear colorless glass was only gradually perfected centuries later. Just how these windows impressed early viewers we can only surmise. For one chronicler their significance seems to have been purely utilitarian; he notes simply that the new glass windows installed in York Minster in the year 669 were an improvement because they "excluded the birds and rain and yet admitted the light."[1] But in some minds at least, such rudimentary stained-glass windows must have evoked the profoundly ambiguous connotations with which all windows remained imbued, however obscurely, to this day. On the one hand, they were a drafty concession to the not infrequently hostile world outside, made in order to purchase the necessary minimum of daylight; on the other hand, they could not help but derive a distinct positive significance from being the source of that light. Never are we more drawn to light, nor does light seem more life-giving, than when we are forced to make do on a miserly amount of it in some light-starved space, such as the buildings of that time typically were. Nowhere is this double-edged meaning more graphically evoked than in the old Norse word from which the English word "window" is derived: *vindauga*, which means literally "wind eye."

The great age of stained glass begins with the classic synthesis of the stained-glass window and architecture in the choir of St-Denis, c. 1140, and ends with the apotheosis of stained glass as a major formative element in the architecture of the Sainte Chapelle in Paris (page 99) just a century later. Confronted with the wealth of imagery in the great cathedral windows of this period, we are inclined to forget that men like the Abbot Suger were drawn to stained glass not alone by the subjects it could depict — in this respect, after all, it was no more versatile than any other art — but by the fact that, in von Simson's words, "the stained-glass window seemingly denies the impenetrable

14. S. Apollinare in Classe, Ravenna, c. 530 A.D.
15. Amiens Cathedral, 1218-47.

Right: 16. *St. Luke,* Codex 51, St. Gall, c. 750 A.D. Stiftsbibliothek, St. Gall.

nature of matter, receiving its visual existence from an energy that transcends it. Light, which is ordinarily concealed by matter, appears as the active principle; and matter is aesthetically real only insofar as it pertakes of, and is defined by, the luminous quality of light."[2] Thus for Suger the light admitted by the stained-glass windows of his church seemed miraculous; and it was this immediate, pre-iconographic quality of the medium itself that, according to von Simson, was one of the chief inspirations for Suger's invention of the Gothic: "In the use he made of the stained-glass window Suger did no more and no less than to give compelling force to an image that was known to all. That is precisely what every great artist or poet does. Suger was the first to conceive his windows not as wall openings but as translucent surfaces to be adorned with sacred paintings. This dual 'invention' distinguished Suger's style from Romanesque and is indeed the basic novelty of Gothic architecture."[3]

Suger died in 1151. By the time that Gothic Chartres was built half a century later, this new architectural order had assumed an absolute authority over all narrative imagery, whether in stained glass or fresco, sculpture or any of the other architectural arts. Their traditional iconography had been superseded in importance by a new and far more ambitious if esoteric symbolism: belief that in the cathedral structure itself, in the radiant, rational and harmonious ordering of all its parts, was a true exemplar of the cosmic order. In this new order the age-old subjects would continue to play an important part — but only as a kind of architectural *leitmotif*. No pictorial subject however central to the dogma is any longer considered potent enough to claim for itself the privileged status of size and centrality of the great mosaic and fresco Pantocrators in the domes and apses of Early Christian, Byzantine and Romanesque

Left: 17. The Alfred Jewel, cloisonné enamel, probably 9th century, Ashmolean Museum.

18. Stucco window grille from the palace of Khirbat al-Mafjeh, Jordan Valley, c. 743 A.D., Palestine Archeological Museum.

churches. The stained glass becomes a magnificently orchestrated spectacle from which we are able to detach ourselves only momentarily to attend to any particular subject.

Intelligible or not, the cathedral windows would continue for a time to tell their stories with the same consummate combination of hieratic dignity, expressive ardor and ornamental ingenuity that characterizes the greatest Romanesque art — of which stained glass was in many respects the most durable offspring. But finally in the Sainte Chapelle, not only are the subjects dissolved into the windows, the individual windows themselves are dissolved into the continuous wall of glass that surrounds three sides of the building. The stained glass *is* the wall, and the viewer finds himself possessed by a luminous energy that seems almost animate.

How can we categorize such an art form without impoverishing it? The more one studies stained glass the more obvious it becomes that this is not "primarily" a pictorial, nor "merely" an ornamental, nor even for that matter "essentially" a Christian art form. To be sure, it is inconceivable apart from the painting, the architecture and the general ethos of the medieval Church — but no more so than it is inconceivable apart from the many skills of the blacksmiths, glassblowers, jewelers and manuscript illuminators that were incorporated into it; or apart from the ornamental genius of the non-Classical world. Indeed, the early cathedral windows owe every bit as much to the world of the endlessly proliferating interlace, the paradoxical figure-and-ground inversion — the fatalistically kinetic rhythms that seem almost to have been the central preoccupation of art from Ireland to the Caucasus — as they do to the monumental style of the Italo-Byzantines. And yet it is no mere conglomerate of all these things either. No matter how deeply we probe into the origins of stained glass or wonder over its strange evolution we are always brought back finally to a single phenomenon: *translucency* in all of its expressive ramifications, however variously these may be interpreted.

Not only is stained glass, like jewelry, animated by the play of light; its principal material, handblown glass, presents us with the same unusual combination of qualities as precious stones: a highly impersonal yet immediately affective beauty that is inherent in the material itself. Whereas the material richness of a fine "painterly" painting is always clearly an achieved quality that bears the unmistakable traces of the artist's own distinctive touch, the richness of gems and colored glass appears to be given as it were by nature. And here, incidentally, we come to the most plausible ground for contending that stained glass is a minor art. If even the simplest pattern of colored glass in a window opening is able because of its intrinsic beauty and the pervasiveness of its aura to create a distinct visual mood; if even the most powerfully composed stained-glass window is at all times so throughly a creature of the play of natural light — and all of this we have maintained — have we not unwittingly confessed that stained glass is really a very minor art after all? An art scarcely more worthy of the name than such captivating but wholly natural phenomena as the play of flames in a fire or waves on the seashore?

The saving difference is that light, unlike these other pleasurable phenomena, *is manipulable by the artist* once he has mastered the various techniques of stained glass. To recognize the primacy of light is therefore in no way to delimit the art. On the contrary; far from having fatally circumscribed the art of stained glass we have simply put ourselves in a position to understand why it must exploit the basic repertoire of formal and expressive devices common to all of the visual arts *in its own way, to its own ends,* which in several respects are unique. Whereas the painter in oils or water color must achieve an effect of richness, the stained-glass artist begins with richness and must work fully as hard to achieve a no less eloquent sobriety. Whereas the painter begins with an opaque surface upon which he may create an abstract or illusory "space," the stained-glass artist starts with an actual void in a real architectural space that he must span with a translucent surface. And whereas the painter in creating his illusory space also creates, however implicitly, some kind of luminous order or "atmosphere" within his painting, the stained-glass artist begins with an actual luminous environment that he modulates so as to create an expressive atmosphere in a real space. Whatever else he may do he is always first of all coloring, refracting, obscuring and fragmenting the light that will pass through his window.

As we have already seen, architecture to a very large extent determines how luminous a stained-glass window *can* be: the darker the interior space the more brilliant by contrast will the light entering its windows appear to our dark-adapted eyes to be; and vice versa. In a greenhouse, for example, where the difference between inside and outside light levels is negligible, the potentiality for luminosity is almost non-existent. The most radiant windows of the 12th century, mounted in such a setting, would probably look more like slate than stained glass. Hence we can see why the basic relation between the stained-glass window and its setting has always necessarily been *dark-to-dark and light-to-light.* Given the brilliant, even harsh light produced by the cavernous interiors of the 12th and early 13th centuries, the early glassworkers very logically composed their windows from a palette of dense, rich colors; or where only clear glass could be employed they painted the glass with a fine ornamental pattern of colorless lines and hatching, or "grisaille," that effectively breaks up and subdues the light.[4]

Later, as the walls of the High and Late Gothic churches were opened up to admit more and more light, the difference between outside and inside light levels was no longer great enough to illuminate the deep ruby-and-blue color harmonies of the 12th and 13th centuries. It was therefore necessary to work out a far lighter palette of tints and secondary colors, and in the gold-and-silvery loveliness of the English parish church windows of the 15th century we can see the logical culmination of this development: an intimate, lyrical, even introspective stained glass, clearly addressed far more to the individual than to an assembled ecclesia, but still perfectly attuned to its architectural setting.

The exceptional instances when medieval stained glass was not so attuned are almost equally instructive. The Sainte Chapelle, for example, is so precociously light and airy that it strains the typical stained-glass palette of the mid-13th century to its limits. Thus, the midday sun streaming through the south windows is often enough to mar the effect of the glass on the north side of the chapel. As the light increases in intensity the painted areas, bars and armatures of the north windows, which function so admirably in silhouette, all begin to seem busily obtrusive. The rubies and blues in these windows lose all of their fire, and as the light picks up the bloom of dust and erosion on the inside of the glass they begin to take on a weak, grayish pallor. It is hard for the inexperienced viewer, seeing them thus for the first time, to realize that they have not somehow "faded."

In Chartres he may observe an instance of the opposite failing, a group of windows that are basically too light for their setting. Some two hundred years after the completion of the cathedral the Vendome Chapel was built into the south aisle of the nave and glazed with windows that, typical of the later period, are considerably lighter than the original glass of the cathedral. Hence, when first encountered on a bright sunny day in the otherwise almost sepulchral atmosphere of the cathedral, these windows seem almost stridently bright and glaring. It is only when one walks right up to them that, shutting out all else and allowing one's eyes to become adapted to their light level, one can enjoy the Vendome windows as the very creditable works of their time which they are.

In sum, the appearance of a stained-glass window is always radically affected by whatever is actually *there* in the overall luminous environment of which it is a part. Change any element in that luminous environment, whether it be the position of the sun and clouds, or the light-transmitting qualities of an adjacent window, and you change the effect of the whole. The myth that the radiance of the old windows is somehow inherent in the glass itself — a product of some wondrous lost glass-coloring *technique* — is simply the persistent mechanical bias of a grossly mechanical civilization.

PART TWO: THE CLAIMS OF THE MEDIUM

The logic of the eye, with its need for balance and symmetry, is not necessarily in agreement with the logic of structure, which in turn is not the logic of pure intellect.

— Henri Focillon

V Radiance

If the radiance of the stained-glass window is far more a product of particular light conditions than of singular materials, it nevertheless remains to determine how the physical window itself actually enters into the creation of this effect. In attempting to do so we shall concentrate our attention upon the west windows of Chartres, an ensemble of 12th-century stained glass whose radiance, unusual even in Chartres, has long been the subject of critical speculation. For reasons that will quickly become apparent, these windows confront the viewer with all of the most difficult problems of aesthetic interpretation in their most beguilingly beautiful form. For an analysis of this kind they are therefore a classic test case.

Even before their recent controversial cleaning the west windows had seemed to glow with an almost uncanny brilliance, as if they alone, of all the windows in the cathedral, had truly captured the sun. Undoubtedly, this was due in part to the fact that the 12th-century blue was generally a far more brilliant color than that of the 13th century, visible in the west rose directly above the three early lancets (page 98); but these had long been notable for still another unusual quality. When viewed from the comparatively short distance of sixty or seventy feet they revealed a full palette of colors: ruby in counterpoint with the predominant blue, with rich secondary accents of gold, green, wine, white and a tawny flesh tint. As one moved further back, however, these windows appeared to become distinctly bluer and lighter in their overall effect, and the other colors, much reduced in intensity, seemed almost to dissolve in the ethereal blueness of the ensemble.

More than anything else it must have been this unusual phenomenon that launched Viollet-le-Duc on this theory of the differential "radiation" of colors in stained glass, a theory that was to reign almost unchallenged for a century. According to this theory, elaborately developed and expounded in his article "Vitrail,"[1] colors in stained glass differ from opaque colors in that they, unlike the latter, have distinct "radiation" properties. Cold colors, and blue above all, have a positive halation. Thus blue color areas in a stained-glass window will always tend to encroach upon and overpower all others, the more so the purer the color and the greater the distance from which it is seen. Warm colors on the other hand, and especially ruby, have the opposite effect, tending to contract within themselves so to speak, under the same condition, which makes them unusually susceptible to being overpowered by blue. Only because the artisans of the Middle Ages somehow discovered this volatile property of colored light and developed an ingenious repertoire of devices to control and actually exploit it, argued Viollet-le-Duc, were they able to create their magnificent stained-glass windows. And only insofar as we for our part recognize and accept this "immutable law of optics" will we again be able to master the art of stained glass.

Not only did this theory seem to account very adequately for the blue dominance of the west windows, which was there for all to see; it was obvious to any impartial observer that few if any of the countless Gothic Revival windows created from the early 1800's on had ever even remotely approached the luminous color harmonies of the ancient glass. That this should have continued to be the case even after the manufacture of an excellent handblown "antique" glass began to be revived during the middle years of the century must have seemed doubly perplexing to successive generations of neo-Gothic stained-glass designers. Little wonder then that "Vitrail," which seemed to describe the hazards and complexities of working with this art form more thoroughly than anything else that had ever been written, came generally to be accepted as the glassman's "bible."

And yet a careful examination of the west windows reveals that they were not painted according to any strict color principle at all. In the *Jesse Tree*, for example, which Viollet-le-Duc used to illustrate his text, the primary blue background is indeed unpainted in seeming accord with the principles set forth in "Vitrail," and the figures deployed against that blue background, from the dormant ruby-robed Jesse at the base to the superb Christ in ruddy purple attire at the top, are painted in the manner described by Viollet-le-Duc and illustrated in his Figure 5.[2] Flanking each of these central figures, however, is a pair of subsidiary figures that are deployed against a *ruby* background and garbed in robes of blue; and here Viollet-le-Duc's formula breaks down. It is the blues that are painted while the rubies are not. In short, the painting on these windows seems to have had little to do with controlling color radiation at all, but appears rather to have been based upon a purely formal principle: whatever color — blue, ruby or occasionally green — functions as the background color for all or part of a window is nearly always left unpainted; wherever that same color is employed in a figurative context it is painted strictly according to the dictates of its subject matter. To assume otherwise is to attribute to early glass painting a thoroughly "cosmetic" function that it did not acquire until centuries later; and to ignore the marvelous adjustment of hue, value and color intensity that quite evidently was achieved *in the glass itself,* prior to the lifting of a brush.

Recently, James R. Johnson did what no one apparently had ever thought to do before: tested one of the key theoretical propositions in "Vitrail" — tested it and found it wanting. In his book *The Radiance of Chartres* Johnson tells us that he had a stained-glass panel made as nearly as possible like the one shown in Viollet-le-Duc's Figure 2 and viewed it at the prescribed distances in company with several colleagues. Neither he nor any of them could detect any of the effects of color radiation that, according to the author of "Vitrail," they should have been able to see. On the strength of this experiment Johnson concluded that Viollet-le-Duc's "views concerning the distinctive irradiating

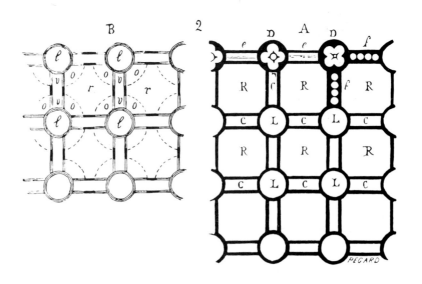

19. and 20. Figure 5 and 2 from "Vitrail."

power of blues, without qualification as to brightness or any other determining factor, have no bases in accepted scientific theory — then or now."[3] While we cannot be too grateful to Mr. Johnson for this critical reassessment of Viollet-le-Duc's theories we are left with the very real problems that Viollet-le-Duc sought to resolve. The singular behavior of the blues in the west windows was beyond dispute just what his theories would lead one to expect; and to this day one sees very few successful red-and-blue windows, whether neo-Gothic or purely contemporary in style. Thus Johnson's experiment leaves totally unresolved the question whether glasspainting performed any indispensable light-modulating function in the early windows at all, or is there purely as illustration and superb calligraphic ornament.

Both in the statement already quoted and even more explicitly in the following one, Johnson suggests a possible explanation for the blue-dominance of the west windows that unaccountably he does not pursue: "There is little reason to believe ... that one color, as such, has a greater tendency to spread than another color, but this would certainly occur if that color were appreciably *brighter* than adjacent colors, containing (or letting through) a greater *amount* of light. Therefore, especially in the case of transparent or translucent color, any spectral hue could irradiate more than the others if it exceeded them in brightness."[4] On the matter of the actual overall brightness of the cathedral windows he is curiously oblique. He contrasts the full brilliance of direct sunlight, which is between 8,000 and 10,000 foot-candles, with the very low light levels that one normally encounters inside the cathedral; but except for one brief excursus about the brightness of a hypothetical stained-glass panel containing clear glass and viewed against a hazy sun of 4,000 foot-candles — a highly atypical example to say the least — he gives us no clue as to the amount of light that normally passes through the west windows or indeed any other actual windows in the cathedral. To anyone who has not himself independently studied the matter such figures are bound to give a very misleading impression.

Like most stained-glass windows most of the time, the west windows in Chartres are viewed not against the direct rays of the sun but rather against the sky, and even the most luminous sky is only a fraction as bright as the sun itself. On a brilliant sunny late September morning in Chartres, for example, the deep blue sky straight overhead measured only two hundred foot-candles; the same thing, surprisingly enough, on the following day which was heavily overcast. The day after that, which was more lightly overcast, gave me my highest reading: eight hundred foot-candles. This morning in New York as I am writing the hazy north sky also has a brightness of about two hundred foot-candles. Of that full sky brightness stained-glass windows, and especially the deeply hued and heavily eroded windows of the 12th and 13th centuries, transmit only a very small portion. On that sunny morning in Chartres, prior to their recent cleaning, the west windows transmitted a mere *three* foot-candles! By contrast, the exterior stonework of the south facade, seemingly so mellow in the full sunlight, measured four hundred foot-candles. That both of these

Pages 48 and 49: 21. and 22. Two photographs taken in Chartres under the same light conditions: average brightness of light reflected from the stonework approximately 400 foot-candles; average brightness of light transmitted by the west windows approximately *three* foot-candles.

light readings were essentially correct is proven by the photographs that I took on that occasion, reproduced on pages 48 and 49.

Nor is the range of brightness values within the early windows as great as one might assume. In the *Becket* panel in Canterbury a white in Becket's lower garment measured five foot-candles while a piece of ruby just beneath it measured approximately one-half a foot-candle. The values of all the other colors lay between these two extremes: the blue background of the panel and the green in the upper part of the saint's garb both measured approximately one foot-candle, the pink on his knee about one-and-a-half. The range of the brightness in this panel therefore exactly corresponds to that which Ansel Adams gives for a "strong painting": one to ten. In the southeast aisle window of All Saints Church, North Street, York, which had recently been cleaned, a clear unpainted white measured two hundred foot-candles, a dark blue thirteen, a light blue fifty, a ruby ten. Even in this much higher-keyed 15th-century work therefore, we find an extreme ratio of only about one to twenty between the lightest and darkest colors. This is less than half the value contrast that one may find in a glossy black-and-white photograph, which according to Adams may run as high as one to fifty. The contrast in a perfectly normal outdoor situation that he describes is far, far greater: "From my window I see a bright painted house in sunlight and some earth under a nearby plant in shade. The brightness range as determined by the S.E.I. meter is 1 : 2,500!"[5] Clearly then, it is neither the absolute brightness of the medieval windows nor the brightness range of the various colors within them that accounts for their singular effect.

During the course of my own study of the west windows I began to realize that although the three windows as an ensemble did appear to become bluer when viewed from greater distances, it was the blue glass alone that stood out in absolute clarity in panel after panel, even when these windows were viewed from as close as possible, with binoculars. On one particularly gloomy afternoon nearly all that one saw, particularly in the upper part of the *Life of Christ* window was black and white and blue. This impression was later confirmed by the color photograph, illustrated on page 98, that I took under far better light conditions: a clear morning sky. I then began to study these same panels from the outside, where the disposition of patina on ancient glass is fairly easy to determine even from a distance, because of its distinctive ashen gray, stonelike surface (page 52). I discovered that not only in the *Life of Christ* but throughout the entire ensemble of 12th-century glass one could quite easily distinguish the blues from the other colors, for it was only the blues that were consistently darker in appearance — and therefore less covered with patina — than the rest of the glass. It became apparent that when these windows were new and all of the colors in them were as clear as the blues still are that they probably were not "blue" windows at all, even when seen from a great distance, but rather had the more sunlit cast that was visible in the lower and less eroded panels of the *Life of Christ*. What I could only surmise the recent cleaning and restoration of these windows appears now to have confirmed: the legendary blueness of the west windows was to a very large extent an inadvertent glory, a product of the more advanced deterioration of the other colors.[6]

Yet when one attempts to account for the singular vivacity of these windows one can only point to certain other qualities which they and they alone have all along possessed and for which no blind force of nature could possibly account. First of all, the particular *combination* of ruby and blue in them is unique. As Johnson noted, the 12th-century ruby contains a higher orange component than that of the 13th century. On the evidence of our eyes, the early blue is also a far purer, more saturated color than any of the later blues in Chartres which, however saturated they may be in comparison with 14th- and 15th-century colors, are quite subtly muted with overtones of purple, gray-green and the like. The 12th-century combination of ruby and blue therefore approaches far more nearly the maximum possible cold-warm polarity of a slightly yellowish red and a slightly greenish blue than any later combination of these two colors. And the law of simultaneous contrast would operate to reinforce this effect even further, according to the color theorist Paul Renner: "If one places the perfect red alongside the perfect blue, the blue takes on some of the complementary color of the red — it therefore becomes greener; and the red assumes something of the complementary of the blue; it becomes yellower ... this change of color direction represents an uncommon increase in the opposition of warm and cold."[7] The west windows are a kind of tour-de-force exploitation of that polarity.

Secondly, we know that these windows were designed to be seen from close at hand. Originally they had opened not into the church proper but into the upper story of a narthex that filled the space between the west towers and in which they must have been seen more or less at eye level, and at quite close range. Thus they were never intended to be clerestory windows at all, but were in fact prototypes of the aisle windows that literally had the floor pulled out from underneath them. Deprived of the chapel-sized space appropriate to the scale of their narrative medallions[8] and situated so they must be viewed from distances of sixty to eighty feet or more, within the whole vast expanse of the cathedral, their original didactic function was clearly sacrificed to the architect's vision of the cathedral as one great unified interior space.

Still another quality that sets them apart from the rest of the windows is the overall character of their composition. One need only to compare them with any of the later medallion windows to realize how very Romanesque "baroque" they are (page 55). To confront this great ensemble of stained glass as it had always been viewed until modern times — sans binoculars and all of the rest of our visual aids — is to be impressed first of all by an extraordinary physical spectacle: a scintillating constellation of ruby-on-blue and blue-on-ruby pattern inversions of almost Celtic or Persian complexity, in which the half-recognized imagery of the individual medallions is all but engulfed. Nowhere is the eye permitted to linger over any detail; rather, it is urged on by a vast tide of visual energy. Radiant, diaphonous, fairly breathing the moods of the sky; the effect is so immediate, so all-pervasive, and so entrancing that any concern with doctrine or dogma seems utterly superfluous. One does not

24. *King Herod and the Scribes*, photographed prior to re-installation after World War II.

Left: 23. The west windows, exterior, prior to cleaning, showing the patina on the glass.

have to be told that he is in the presence of the sublime. How effective such a charged repetition of elements by itself can be may be seen in the remarkable windows that Anton Wendling created for the Gothic choir in Aachen shortly after World War II. Employing nothing but a quartered circle within a circle within a square, and an extremely telling sequence of color changes in these eighty-foot lancets, he has demonstrated as no one before him the affinity between the most modern idiom and Gothic fenestration on a grand scale.

How then are we finally to assess the role of painting in these windows? Must we conclude that it contributes nothing to their overall effect, that it is nothing more nor less than a superb vehicle for the rendition of their subjects? Obviously, since the glasspainting of the 12th and 13th centuries was essentially linear, it could not and did not attempt to modulate color *or* value. Nor was it employed to delineate the major elements of the composition even within a single narrative roundel. All of these are defined and bounded by the leading and iron armatures. The one thing that it undoubtedly could and did do was to fragment the light passing through the glass, and it remains only to determine what effect this has on the overall appearance of the windows. And here it seems to me that Viollet-le-Duc, for all of his mistaken theories, was very close to the truth. He was very aware that flat tones painted on glass as they were in the 16th and 17th centuries, without relief, without either the support of an intelligible lead pattern or any clear-cut linear or refractory contrasts, tend to create a deadly dull and lifeless effect, whereas the constantly reiterated lines of early glasspainting, "disclosing the local colors of the glass between them," creates an extraordinarily vibrant effect. To be convinced of this fact one need only to observe the effects of light fragmentation elsewhere — in nature, in the age-old lattice-work windows of the Near and Far East (page 187), and most importantly in the best contemporary German stained glass. That the highly linear composition of the early windows was deliberate we can hardly doubt, for despite the many similarities between early Gothic manuscript illumination, fresco and glasspainting, it is only in stained glass that the painted line, consistently echoing, articulating and ornamenting the principal forms delineated by the leads, appears as an almost invariable style. Long before we are able to identify the imagery of an ancient window or are close enough to delight in the bravura of its calligraphy, we are captivated by a sense of inexhaustible *richness,* of such subtlety and intricacy that it can hardly be attributed to color alone; and this is surely due in no small part to the almost capillary light-screening action of its painting. But before we can really assess the effect of glasspainting we must take a closer look at the surface to which that painting is affixed: the glass itself.

Right: 25. *Good Samaritan* window, Chartres, c. 1225. 26. *Life of Christ* window, Chartres, c. 1155. 27. Anton Wendling: Choir window, Aachen Cathedral, 1951.

Page 56: 28. The capillary light-screening action of bare branches.

Page 57: 29. Maria Katzgrau: Friedens Evangelical Church, Baesweiler.

VI *The Texture of Light*

Although stained glass is nominally a two-dimensional art form and to that extent a mode of painting, it has a very significant third-dimensional quality that radically distinguishes it from either painting or sculpture: it is always vitally engaged with the luminous visual field *behind* it. That is to say, we always see *through* it to a greater or lesser degree, even when we think that we are simply looking *at* it. To a far greater extent than is generally recognized even by perceptive viewers, the appearance of the stained-glass window is a product of the various light-modulating elements beyond the window itself and more or less directly in the viewer's line of vision. These can either emphasize or totally obscure certain of the most distinctive qualities of the glass itself. Only to the degree that the viewer understands this — perceives just what, in, on and beyond the surface of the glass determines its appearance in any given situation, and how one might alter either the glass or its luminous environment to obtain some other desired effect — can he be said to understand the language of stained glass. An example should help to make this clear.

In my bathroom hangs a small ornamental panel that is largely transparent and contains no glasspainting at all; nothing to arrest the eye at the surface of the glass except the color and texture of the glass itself. Normally it is seen against a nondescript visual mish-mash of buildings bedecked with fire escapes, clotheslines and other backyard paraphenalia. But as it happens, this commonplace background could hardly be more flattering to the glass, for it is largely due to it that the panel normally shimmers and sparkles as it does in the photograph opposite. The photograph on page 61 shows the same panel just a few moments later — in the same setting, photographed from the same angle and with the same exposure — but after both it and the clear window glass behind it had been fogged up by condensation from the shower. All of its "glassiest" qualities have been effectively obscured and with them much of the point of the work. One could hardly hope for a more eloquent demonstration of the difference between transparency and translucency, already insisted upon in Chapter II. As we noted there, light rays passing through a denser-than-air medium like glass or water are always refracted, which is to say deflected to a greater or lesser degree, by undulations in the surface of that medium. Hence every variation in the surface of this panel, whether it be the bold geometric facets of the pressed-glass ornaments or the minute surface irregularities of the handblown glass, actually functions like a tiny distorting lens, picking up and transmitting to the viewer some more or less radically displaced aspect of whatever lies beyond the glass. However, it is only when

Right and page 61: 30. and 31. Robert Sowers: *Farewell to Franklin Street*, 1970; detail, showing the effects of variegated and diffused light.

58

this background contains a range of discrete elements both darker and lighter than the average tonality of the glass itself that this optically rich scramble of refractory activity *can be seen.* When viewed against the diffused light of the steamed up window, and with its own surfaces steamed up as well, all of this is lost.

In sum, the stained-glass artist's "canvas," if it may be called that even in quotation marks, is never neutral or quiescent, never the product of his glass or his light source alone. It is always a highly volatile interaction between the two. Change either and the other is radically affected.

If we now examine the surface of a medieval window like the *Ezekiel* panel reproduced on page 77, it should be obvious why ancient glass is less ravaged by flat lighting than most more recent windows. Not only are the ancient windows typically more fragmented with leading and magnificently painted details, but their surface is neither wholly transparent nor wholly translucent. Rather, it is usually covered with a patina of almost microscopic scratches and erosion which have a distinctive optical richness of their own. Although this patina is by its nature hard to photograph, some sense of it can be gained from this very excellent full-sized detail. What such windows have lost in transparency they have gained in a kind of graphic venerability to which we find it hard not to respond; it is no more nor less than the dirt of the ages; but we should remember that this quality is both foreign to their conception and only by happy accident as beautiful as it often is. In any case, it is this quality that undoubtedly prevented students of stained glass from recognizing that whatever is beyond a stained-glass window — eaves, trees, shaded or sunlit walls, or the sky in any of its moods — is always to a greater or lesser degree an element in the effect of that window. To be sure, the more transparent the glass the more prominent such background elements become, and the nearer to ground level a window is the more diverse such elements are likely to be; but even the clerestory windows in the cathedrals, eroded though they are with age, are still alive to the slightest movement of sun and clouds as everyone who has ever studied them knows.

But to return to the glass itself: whether by accident or intent the glassmakers of the 12th and 13th centuries produced a material that had almost the ideal refractory properties for stained glass. It was both thin enough and flat enough to be cut into the necessary shapes, yet still irregular enough in thickness to have the kind of rich transitions in depth or tonality of color that are evident, for example, in the background of the *Thadeus* panel illustrated on page 62. With the progress of glass technology in the later Middle Ages and the Renaissance, however, came the ability to produce larger, thinner and flatter sheets of glass — a glass that at each perceptible state in this process of optical refinement became less visually substantial, less intrinsically interesting as a material. Hence the dual phenomenon that at the very same time when glass painting was coming to the fore as the principal carrier of interest in the stained-glass window, the physical fabric of the window was being deprived of one of the chief sources of its earlier richness. Although much of the difference between the quality of earlier and later glass is necessarily lost in photographs, it is

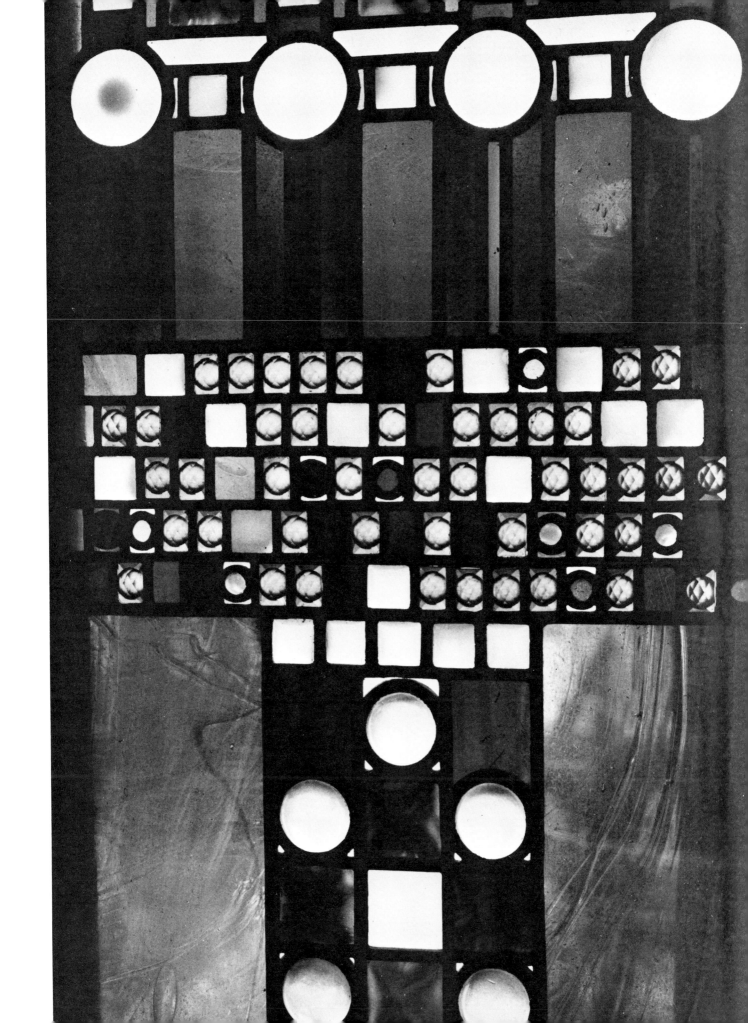

32. *Thadeus,* French, c. 1200, Walters Gallery, Baltimore; detail.

Right: 33. *St. Anne and the Virgin,* Almondbury, Yorkshire, mid-15th century.

Page 64: 34. Ludwig Schaffrath: Cloister window, Aachen cathedral, 1962-65; detail.

Page 65: 35. Robert Sowers: Residential window, Brooklyn, N.Y., 1980.

62

instructive to compare our illustration of a 15th-century *Virgin and St. Ann* with the earlier *Thadeus* panel. Despite the beauty of the later work one can see from the almost undistorted visibility of the protective screening behind it that the glass upon which it is painted is hardly more substantial in appearance than ordinary 19th-century window glass. And indeed, it was not until the 1840's that the Gothic Revivalists began, at the urging of the lawyer and nonpareil amateur Charles Winston, to revive the glassmaking techniques of the earlier period. It is thanks to their efforts that our modern handblown "antique" glass is remarkably similar to the best glass in the cathedrals.

Following Winston's lead, subsequent technology has worked to the great advantage of the stained-glass artist, producing a whole variety of colors, textures and other valuable qualities that were completely unknown in the Middle Ages. To enumerate the most important of these, there is first of all "seedy" antique, which is simply a very bubbly handblown glass. Because the bubbles catch and scatter the light they make this glass less transparent without making it less lively — a most useful property, as may be seen in the work illustrated on page 64. Second, there is "reamy" antique, in which all of the typical irregularities of handblown glass are deliberately emphasized. The contrasting effect of seedy and reamy antique alongside clear window glass is apparent in the photograph on page 65. Third, and perhaps most important of all are the various types of "flashed" glass, which are laminates of two different colors or kinds of glass. Flashed colors on a clear base often have a particular clarity because the color layer itself is almost paper-thin, a tiny fraction of the approximately eighth-of-an-inch thickness of the base glass to which it is fused. Or where one color is flashed upon the tint of another, such as ultramarine on a pale yellow, it may have a fine indefinable subtlety. And flashed glass may in addition be seedy, reamy or "streaky," in which latter case the flash runs irregularly thick and thin on the base, producing a moderate, extreme or deliberately exotic variety of striation and shading in its *color*. Where a ruby flash runs thin on a greenish base, for example, one may get a marvelous range of autumnal colors that are neither red nor green; on a bluish base a similar range of strange melancholy violets and rose madders; often useful. But flashed glass has certain other important properties significant enough to demand a paragraph of their own.

First of all, because flashed glass is a laminate of two colors, the artist is able by removing any degree or part of the flash to work with combinations of both colors on a single piece of glass, without the intermediation of a leadline. Of this technique, which was first systematically exploited by the glasspainters of the later Middle Ages, more will be said in the next chapter. But flashing makes possible still another very interesting range of qualities and it is these that concern us here. If a glass is flashed, not with another clear color but with a film of opal or milk glass, two things happen: depending upon the thickness of the flash the glass becomes to a greater or lesser degree translucent rather than transparent — permanently "fogged"; and a small fraction of the base glass color is reflected back toward the light source, thus becoming visible on the *exterior* of the window. Both of these qualities serve to give the glass

Right: 36. David Wilson: Our Lady of Perpetual Help Chapel, Atlanta, 1973; and 37. St. Gabriel's Monastery, Brighton, Massachusetts, 1967.

Right: 38. Ludwig Schaffrath: Prism window, Papst-Johannes-Haus, Krefeld, 1968; detail.

a tangible surface interest and have been very effectively exploited in Germany where this type of glass was developed. On an architectural scale the kind of refractory activity that was so effective in our first example can be quite overwhelming, and the various opal-flashes provide the artist with a ready means of controlling them. But even on a small scale they may be employed as an effective foil to other more lively types of glass. Also, the muted hint of color on the exterior often comes as a welcome relief to the comparative starkness of most contemporary architecture. Where a strong exterior color is desired, however, that also can be achieved. For when a thin film of transparent color is flashed upon an opal base the full strength of that color will be reflected back toward the light source and so be visible from the outside, as may be seen in David Wilson's Atlanta window. Indeed, by combining the various types of glass at his disposal in varying proportions the artist can actually "reverse" the stained-glass window to whatever degree he wants.

The fourth type of glass that we must consider is not handblown but machine-pressed or rolled. In this category I include everything from the turn-of-the-century ornaments in my bathroom panel, to the ribbed and mechanically textured glass that one normally associates with office partitions and shower doors, to the cast prisms that Ludwig Schaffrath designed for himself in the mid-1960's, illustrated opposite. When judiciously combined with handblown glass even the most austere ribbed glass can be surprisingly effective, as David Wilson's Brighton monastery window on page 67 demonstrates.

Finally, there is cast slab glass, a massive inch-thick material that was first developed by the French about 1930. Because it is roughly five or six times as thick as antique glass, and because of its rough-cast surfaces, even clear slab glass has a very substantial appearance, which the glazier may further accentuate by flaking the edges of each individual piece as he cuts it. For this reason many people have come to feel that slab glass is the most "contemporary" or the most "architectural" form of stained glass, but it is important to understand why there really is no such thing as *the* best technique except in relation to a particular kind of architectural setting, range of light conditions, artistic concerns. Without question slab glass has greatly extended the expressive range of the medium in the direction of sheer massiveness. Since the slab-glass panel is itself a piece of masonry it easily and naturally takes its place in the masonry wall as a logical part of it. Slab glass is certainly the most romantically "brutalist" form of stained glass, with all of the most accidental, raw-material aspects of the medium to the fore. How effective it can be in the hands of an artist with a sufficiently strong design sense the Buschulte and Schaffrath windows on pages 70 and 71 make clear. Unfortunately, however, this technique has been seized upon by the worst Disneyland medievalists of the trade to lend a kind of spurious modernity to their work — modernity being equated with crudity. But the real limitations of slab glass are the price that one pays for its chief virtue, its visual substantiality.

Since slab glass is so massive it cannot possibly have the same liquid clarity and delicacy as antique glass, nor can it exploit any of the contrasting effects of transparency and translucency that may be created even on a piece of plain

Page 70: 39. Wilhelm Buschulte: Trial panel for windows in St. Clemens, Drolshagen.

Page 71: 40. Ludwig Schaffrath: St. Mathew's Church, Leverkusen-Fettehenne, 1966-67.

Page 72: 41. Victorian doorlight, Brooklyn, N.Y.; detail.

Page 73: 42. Ludwig Schaffrath: Maria Immaculata, Neersen.

window glass. In order to appreciate this one need only to recall the rich variety of effects achieved in Victorian etched, cut, sandblasted and embossed glass through the manipulation of just those qualities alone. Notice, in our example, how the translucent field of frosted glass underlying the floral motifs tends to hold its middle tone value in spite of the extreme light changes outside, while the design embossed upon it, which is much more nearly transparent, takes on the tonality of whatever lies directly behind it. In the center of the panel the embossed floral motifs thus read as light-on dark, while at the edges they read as dark-on-light; and in the presence of the actual panel this reversal has no fixed position but as many variations as the ever-shifting play of light outside and the movement of the viewer inside can give it. This same vibrant, airy "chiaroscuro" is at the disposal of the contemporary stained-glass artist once he learns how to play off the relatively static effects of translucent glass — whether painted, etched sandblasted or opal-flashed — against the mercurial variability of transparent glass. For the first time in centuries no barrier of taste or technique prevents him from employing this quality as a major expressive device, as Schaffrath demonstrated in his superb if short-lived entrance wall in Neerson, the unaccountable victim of a renovation.

VII *The Fabric of a Stained-Glass Window*

Contrary to widespread opinion, the stained-glass artist has little or nothing to do with the actual making or coloring of glass. That is a prior craft, and must already have been so by the latter part of the 12th century. By that time the amount of stained glass required for the new Gothic churches had become so great that the windowmakers found it convenient to set up their workshops near the major building sites, while the glassmakers preferred to remain as near as possible to the sources of sand, potash, lime and firewood that they began to need in greatly increased quantities. Suffice to say that the glass used in making stained-glass windows is colored in exactly the same way as ordinary bottle glass, by the addition of metallic oxides to it while it is in a molten state: cobalt for blue, iron for green, copper for ruby, manganese for purple. Thus the art of stained glass proper begins with a stock of pre-colored sheets of glass as its primary material, much as the art of easel painting begins with tubes of colored paint and canvas, and the term "stained glass" with its connotations of some arcane glass-dying process is grossly misleading. Nor is the German term *Glasmalerei* any better, for it encourages the equally false notion that colors in stained glass are somehow *painted* — as if the stained-glass artist were the manipulator of some kind of gorgeous irradiated molasses. Both terms reflect the same naively mechanistic effort to reduce to a physical material or technique qualities that are almost entirely the product of the interaction between glass and light. In fact, the classic stained-glass window of the 13th century is far more like a translucent mosaic than a painting, as the following diagrams will make clear.

They retrace the basic steps in the making of a typical 13th-century panel, *The Prophet Ezekiel* from a French "Jesse Tree" window:[1] from the design or cartoon (A) a pattern (B) is made, showing the exact shapes and sizes of the pieces of glass to be cut, and indicating the color for each piece: blue for the background, ruby for the halo, flesh tint for the head, and so on. A piece of glass of the appropriate color is selected for each area and cut to shape, allowing a small space between it and all of the adjacent pieces for the leading, as in (C). (See also the unglazed *Thadeus* panel illustrated on page 175.) The details of the design, in this case features, drapery and ornamental motifs, are then painted *onto* the glass more or less opaquely. Sometimes this is done by placing the glass directly over the cartoon and tracing the original design, as in (D). The paint used for this is a relatively colorless vitreous enamel composed of dense brownish, blackish or gray-greenish metal oxides and ground glass, mixed with some purely temporary aqueous glue binder like gum arabic.

43. A, Cartoon

B, Pattern

C, Glass cut to size

D, Glasspainting

E, Glazing

Right: 44. *Ezekiel*, French, 13th century, Victoria & Albert Museum; detail, approximately actual size.

This vitreous enamel, employed here in an almost purely linear fashion, is then "fired" into the surface of the glass by placing the painted pieces into a kiln and heating them to a temperature just sufficient to fuse the paint to the glass. Finally, the pieces are assembled with preformed strips of lead, grooved on either side so as to take the glass (E). These are fitted around all of the pieces of glass and the joints between them soldered. The completed panel is then waterproofed by scrubbing or pressing a putty compound under the leads, and it is ready for installation.

The 9th-century reliquary cover from Séry-les-Mèziéres, probably the oldest stained-glass panel to have survived intact into modern times, shows us how glasspainting initially functioned in relation to the other basic elements of the medium. In this panel the leading, necessary to join the various pieces of yellowish and olive-green glass together, also delineates its principal form. Only the strips of glass that outline the cross have been painted, with an opaque layer of enamel into which the ornamental motif was scratched with a stylus. This is a minimal use of glasspainting to be sure, but already in this modest

45. Reliquary cover, Séry-les-Mèziéres, 9th century.

panel we can see the completely coordinated deployment of colored glass, articulating leadline and painted detail that we find in the fully developed windows of the cathedrals.

From the mid-13th century on, however, as the relationship between stained glass and architecture began to count for less and less, the aims, techniques and achievements of the stained-glass artist began to resemble those of the fresco and easel painter, and increasingly it is by the standards applicable to the latter that the stained glass of the 15th, 16th and 17th centuries must be judged. The first significant developments in the glasspainter's craft appear to have been made more or less simultaneously in the early 14th century. A range of very fine secondary colors — smoky ambers, moss greens and gray violets — became generally available for the first time and, especially in England and France, began to replace ruby and blue as the dominant colors in the windowmaker's palette. The technique of literally staining glass yellow by painting it with silver salts was discovered — the only technique that legitimizes the English-language name of the art; and glasspainters began to develop techniques for shading or modelling forms with their vitreous enamel. Where artists of the 12th and 13th centuries had been content to render halftones in discrete areas, or secondary lines of flat translucent tonality, as for example in the torso of the Canterbury *Adam* illustrated on page 181, there was now a growing concern to render *gradations* of tonality. To this end the glasspainter began to apply a translucent tone to the whole surface of his glass, which he then very delicately brushed away wherever he wished to create a highlight; in order to deepen shadows he would apply secondary coats of glass paint and stipple them into the undercoat. The uses of line became increasingly versatile and delicate, especially in the 15th century, as may be seen in the exquisitely painted *Virgin and Child* in Merton College Chapel.

To these refinements of the craft the 15th century added, or more accurately developed the potentialities of, at least one wholly new technique: the abrasion of "flashed" glass — initially ruby glass, whose unique structure undoubtedly inspired the invention of this technique. Because the metallic agent needed to produce this color is so dense, ruby glass becomes all but opaque except in the thinnest films; hence the early glassblowers had hit upon the ingenious process of "flashing" such a film of ruby onto the surface of a clear white base. What the glasspainters now began to do was to grind away portions of this ruby veneer so as to expose the clear base glass underneath, thus achieving a color change from ruby to white on a single piece of glass. Subsequently other colors were also flashed so that they too could be treated in this manner. To such combinations of a flashed color and white could also be applied the yellow stain already described, as well as the traditional colorless glass paint. In the hands of a master like Peter Hemmel von Andlau (page 100) this repertoire of techniques would become the instrument of an unprecedented versatility *within* the traditional scaffolding of leads, but elsewhere these new techniques would be seen as a means of liberation from what was increasingly coming to be considered the "tyranny" of the leadline.

The success of these new techniques probably encouraged glasspainters to

Page 80: 46. *Virgin and Child*, Fladbury, Worcestershire, first half of 14th century.

Page 81: 47. *Virgin and Child*, Merton College Chapel, Oxford, 15th century.

seek still other means of expanding the painterly resources of their craft. The traditional vitreous enamel was increasingly employed as an overall matt to tone down, or seem to shade the basic color of the glass itself; in the 16th century fragments of colored glass were ground up in an abortive effort to create a full palette of colors that could be freely painted onto clear glass. As late as the 1530's one can observe, in the glasspainting of Valentin Busch for example, a clear appreciation of the cleanly articulated contour, whether painted or scratched out of a painted tone as a highlight — but he was still a bona fide *glass*painter, schooled in the craft and executing windows of his own design. It was only with the abandonment of such devices that his successors, blindly emulating the illusionistic effects of easel painting, began to create the kind of flat parchmentlike tonalities of which Viollet-le-Duc complained: tonalities that "have the great fault of lacking luminosity, and give to interiors a false light, seemingly without depth. In a building permeated with this lamplike light, one feels oppressed."[2]

Although the techniques of cutting glass were notably refined at about this time with the development of the diamond, and subsequently of the steel-wheel glass cutter, and the technique of etching flashed glass with the discovery of hydrofluoric acid, it was not until the revival of the early glassglass-making techniques and the development of the new types of glass, already described in the last chapter, that there were any further artistically significant refinements of the craft. Among these slab glass has most significantly affected the traditional technique of assembling a stained-glass window. Instead of being leaded this inch-thick glass is normally cast into concrete panels of approximately its own thickness, where it functions like a large-scaled translucent aggregate. Two refinements of this technique, which have been most effectively exploited in Germany, are the treatment of the concrete surfaces as a form of low-relief sculpture, as in Poensgen's Bad Honnef windows illustrated on page 116, and Wilhelm Buschulte's novel method of mounting pieces of slab glass on cut-steel plate like hugh cabochons, illustrated on pages 70 and 134.

But before we can properly assess such recent developments in the art of stained glass we must attempt to understand the reasons for its decline, and these must be sought in the stained glass of the 16th, 17th and 18th centuries.

Right: 48. Valentin Busch: *Renée de Bourbon*, Metz Cathedral, 1523. 49. William Peckitt: *Sir Thomas Burnett*, Yorkshire, 18th century, Victoria & Albert Museum.

VIII *Luminous Reality vs. Pictorial Illusion*

If no style, as such, can claim sovereignty over any other — and this I believe most modern critics would agree is axiomatic — then Renaissance stained glass certainly deserves to be judged as it rarely has been judged, without reference to that of the Middle Ages. But it does not follow, as some critics would apparently have us believe, that the stained glass of the two periods served such completely different functions that there are no criteria against which both may be validly measured. Thus it is pure special pleading when John Canaday asserts that "late stained glass is no better nor worse than early, but simply unrelated to it," and his arguments in support of this contention are wrong as a matter of fact. Medieval stained glass, he tells us, was "never meant to be seen at close range," whereas that of the 16th and 17th centuries was "often made for smaller buildings than cathedrals ... where it was intended to be examined closely as a painting for skill of craftsmanship, beauty (usually involving complexity) of detail, and stylishness of design."[1] Although medieval stained glass was certainly designed to be effective when viewed from a distance, not all of it was designed to be viewed *solely* from a distance. The choir aisle windows in Canterbury, for example, are deployed more or less at eye level, as were the west windows of the 12th-century narthex of Chartres; and one would be hard put to find a more spectacular display of craftsmanship, beauty, and sheer proliferation of detail on a vast scale than in these works. Nor, to examine the other side of the coin, was all or even most Renaissance stained glass designed to be examined at close range. From the beginning, c. 1500, until the very end in the New College Chapel windows of Sir Joshua Reynolds, stained glass continued to be made on a monumental as well as an intimate scale. Thus medieval and Renaissance stained glass, far from being "unrelated," served overlapping functions, and even stylistically they were but the two polar extremities of a continuous development in which it is impossible to say where the influence of the one period leaves off and that of the other begins. Stained glass is finally *one* art form, in which all works of whatever style are presumably linked together by certain qualities that they share with no other medium; otherwise the term makes very little sense indeed.

This is not to suggest that the medium itself presents us with a sufficient criterion for measuring the quality of artistic achievement. But given the particular expressive resources of this (or any other) medium one can always observe how a particular artist or culture has chosen to exploit them. And especially when those resources are strained or in some way intentionally delimited, one may ask, if one does not automatically do so: *What has been sacrificed and what*

has been gained? And one may do this without imposing the artistic presuppositions of any particular style upon the art in question. In short, the mere fact that the stained-glass artists of the Renaissance chose not to exploit the same range of qualities that were exploited in the Middle Ages tells us almost nothing about the quality of their achievement; but it leaves wide open the question of what, in a positive sense, they were attempting to do and what they actually *did* do.

In order to grasp their intent one can do no better than to consult their original designs, but before turning to the sketch for a typical monumental window of the 16th century it will be instructive to examine what is generally assumed to be the initial design for a late 12th- or early 13th- century window. Known as the Guthlac Roll, this is a parchment scroll upon which are drawn in line with a few rudimentary touches of color eighteen episodes from the life of St. Guthlac, all in roundels. This scroll is every bit as significant for what it does not contain as for what it does. In it there is no indication of a color scheme, no disposition of leadlines, no hint as to the overall composition of the window; all of this was presumably left to the master glasspainter. But not even the images themselves could have been intended to be executed line for line, because the silhouettes of the figures are far too intricate to have been translated into stained glass without considerable modification. At most,

50. Guthlac Roll, Harley Y6, English, c. 1200, British Museum.

then, the Guthlac Roll could have functioned as a very generalized inspiration — as an illustrated chronology of the saint's life, probably created in some monastic scriptorium for the general instruction of a stained-glass atelier commissioned to produce a window — presumably a medallion window — devoted to St. Guthlac. But what is most significant for our purposes is how much is left to the discretion of the glassworkers: the whole ornamental schema of the window, the color, the size and disposition of the narrative episodes. There is nothing essential to the meaning and spirit of these drawings for which one cannot find a perfectly straightforward solution in the aisle windows of Canterbury or Chartres.

The same cannot be said for Geoffrey Dumonstier's mid-16th-century design, even though it is less worked out in detail than the Guthlac Roll. In this design and absolutely essential to it are two entirely new elements, full three-dimensional space and the illusion of natural light and shade. In a vast space seen, as it were, "through" the mullions of the window, the artist has deployed an ensemble of figures that seem almost sculpturally modeled. All of this is faultlessly managed; Dumonstier clearly knew all that anyone needed to know about the orchestration of a complex subject in the grand manner of the time; but it is a conception for which there is no real equivalent, however technically ingenious, *in stained glass*. For in order to create the illusion of such a vast space, skewing off diagonally into the indeterminate distance, the artist must first of all be able to make the actual physical surface of his image invisible, as such; and this the stained-glass artist simply cannot do. Confronted with the task of translating such an image into stained glass he is bound to find himself frustrated at every turn, not only by the unyielding two-dimensional materiality of his glass, but above all by his leadlines and other structural elements. He is forced to choose between two alternatives, neither of them satisfactory. He can either employ his leadlines in the traditional manner to emphasize the main lines of his design, or he can treat them as nothing more than an unfortunate structural necessity to be employed as sparingly as technically possible. In Romain Buron's *Martyrdom of St. Foy* we can see what happens in either case. Where the leadline is employed in the traditional way to outline the principal contours of the subject, as they are for example in the legs of the principal figure on the left, they tend to flatten him out and pull him back to the surface of the window. Where they do not do so, as in the legs of the executioner, the effect is no less appalling. He looks like a piece of ceramic sculpture from the waist down. Throughout the entire window the legibility and spatial deployment of the subject matter is marred by this same kind of hit-or-miss conflict between leadline and painted contour.

Impossible to illustrate but no less difficult for the stained-glass artist are the problems posed by the need to create an illusion of a light source within, or seeming to play upon the subjects in a three-dimensional space. For generally speaking, the farther the spatial illusion is pushed the more literally the effects of light must be depicted as well; and the more this is done the more nearly such illusory light effects are brought into competition with the real light that actually illuminates the window. Pushed beyond a certain point, the effort

Right: 51. Geoffrey Dumonstier: Design for a stained-glass window, c. 1545, Louvre. 52. Romain Buron: The Martyrdom of St-Foy, Conches, c. 1535.

53. The *Tullier* window, Bourges Cathedral, 1532.

Right: 54. Dirk Vellert: *Gift of the Magis*, Antwerp, 1532, Hessisches Landesmuseum, Darmstadt.

to impose such a static illusion upon the vibrant reality of natural light becomes simply fatuous.

To be sure, not all monumental stained-glass windows of the 16th century succumbed to these errors; but then neither did they attempt to push the spatial illusion anything like so far. In the Bourges *Tullier* window, for example, which is almost exactly contemporary with Buron's *Martyrdom of St. Foy,* the space is considerably flattened or compressed and the figures, architectural setting and blue background are composed in a sequence of planes that are all rigorously parallel to the picture plane of the window itself. Furthermore, the bold changes of color and value in the *Tullier* window are composed in such a way that they absorb the visual impact of the leadlines, thus allowing them to reinforce the main lines of the composition without becoming obtrusive. In short, there appears to be a rather definite, structually determined threshold beyond which the spatial illusion in stained glass *cannot be pushed without compro-*

55. Coat of Arms of the Freyburger Guild, Strasbourg, 1571, Hessisches Landesmuseum, Darmstadt.

56. East window, Church of St. Mary, Battersea, London, 1634.

mising that very illusion. And it takes no medieval bias to observe how the glasspainters of the period increasingly ignored that threshold, to their own detriment, in their Icarus-like ambition to duplicate the representational feats of fresco and easel painters.

Turning now to the miniature, or "close-range" stained glass of the 16th century, we may observe the parallel emergence of two distinct styles, and in them an almost complete split between the pictorial on the one side and the ornamental on the other. The typical pictorial or narrative roundel of the period illustrates the logical, and so far as the art of stained glass is concerned the terminal, development in the effort to turn stained glass into pure painting. In the 16th century the roundel is reduced enough in size so that an entire image can be executed on a single piece of glass. Dirk Vellert's *Adoration* panel, for example, is only slightly more than eleven inches in diameter. Though frequently of the highest quality, such works are pure brush drawings; the fact that they happen to be executed on glass seems almost incidental. Far more interesting from our point of view, therefore, is the simultaneous development of the heraldic panel into a tour-de-force display of all the technical resources of stained glass — brilliantly colored glass, much of it flashed glass that is etched, painted and silver-stained to create the kind of rich, complex effects that one sees in the 1571 coat of arms of the Freyburger Guild in Strasbourg. The best of these panels are marvels of uninhibited ornamental exuberance, beautiful in and of themselves; but they are also interesting for what they seem to tell us about the nature of monumental stained glass.

57. Ghirlandajo: *Circumcision* window, S. Maria Novella, Florence, late 15th century.

58. Coat of Arms of Johannes Jansen, Dutch, 1638, Victoria & Albert Museum.

In St. Mary's Church, Battersea, there is a window dating from c. 1634, with miserably weak portraits in the lower parts of its three lancets; but the window is fairly sustained by the ornamental vigor of the heraldry above. Reproduced side-by-side with the Freyburger Guild panel as it is here, without regard for the difference in size of the two works, this window strongly suggests that whereas there are definite limits to how far the illusion of deep space can be pushed in stained glass, there are no comparable limits to its development as pure ornament. Must we therefore conclude that stained glass is essentially an ornamental art after all? At this point some careful distinctions must be made, as our next illustrations will prove. The first, Ghirlandajo's *Circumcision* window in S. Maria Novella, Florence, is not only a pictorial image but an image in which one of the most prominent motifs is a barrel vault that thrusts forcibly back into space. The second, a Dutch coat of arms of the 17th century, is no less clearly ornamental, and primarily *two*-dimensional in composition. Nevertheless, it is the Ghirlandajo that is legible and stable, and the Dutch work that is not; and the reason is clear. Like the master of the *Tullier* window, Ghirlandajo has composed his *space* frontally and symmetrically, which is to say ornamentally; and he has patterned his darks and lights even more boldly than the French artist in order to establish the necessary bond between the plane delineated by the leadlines and the illusory plane behind it. This is precisely what was not done in the Dutch panel, and why it fails. The contrast between the painted design and the grid of leadlines superimposed upon it is so great that the two cannot possibly meet, with the result that the design

59. Ghiberti: *Prayer in the Garden*, Duomo, Florence, early 15th century.

60. Donatello: *Annunciation*, Duomo, Florence, early 15th century.

seems to hover uncertainly an indeterminate distance "behind" the plane that is established by the leadlines. If one accepts Rudolf Arnheim's definition of disorder as "a clash of uncoordinated orders,"[2] this surely is a textbook example.

These same principles may be seen to apply, though in a far more subtle way, to a pair of windows from a single ensemble: Ghiberti's *Prayer in the Garden* and Donatello's *Coronation of the Virgin* in the Duomo in Florence. In the Ghiberti we see what might be called a melodious distribution of light and dark accents throughout the window; no single figure or other element seeks to arrest the eye for long. But Donatello has sought to monumentalize his two figures as much as possible, and in this he is clearly the more "advanced" artist of the two — a full step closer to the apotheosis of the human figure that was ultimately to be realized by Michelangelo. At the same time, his window is far less happily organized two-dimensionally than Ghiberti's. Evidently ill-at-ease with the leadlines, Donatello has simply run them in continuous horizontal bands except where they are stopped so as not to go lancing through the middle of a face. In contrast to the regular but unassimilated geometry of these leadlines, which here as in the Dutch panel seek to establish their own plane, the distribution of darks and lights across the surface of the window seems completely arbitrary, the predominance of darks on the right making that side of the composition lopsidedly heavy.

To say, then, that stained glass is essentially an ornamental art is to say no more and no less than that *the structure of the stained-glass window must be organized in such a way as to make possible some kind of visually coherent relationship between it and whatever the window seeks to express, whether in two or three dimensions. In the last analysis, its structure and its form are one.* But this is not quite the end of the matter. As we have already seen, the full-blown illusion of space à la Dumonstier is a technical impossibility. This is no mere reiteration of the time-worn dictum, which so many of the greatest wallpainters from Masaccio to Tiepolo managed to do without, that the mural arts "should not violate the integrity of the picture plane." Beyond certain limits stained glass simply *cannot* do so, but let us suppose for the moment that it could. To draw the viewer's attention off into some limitless imaginary space beyond the picture plane would be to ignore one of the most singular attractions of stained glass as a medium, its *aura* — its capacity to transform the actual space in which the viewer finds himself. And that too, I submit, would be fatuous.

Perhaps at this point certain comparisons between the stained glass of the Renaissance and that of the Middle Ages may be fairly ventured. The art of stained glass was very much a medieval invention, an art that followed almost logically from a milieu in which glassblowing, enamelling, goldsmithing and architectural ornamentation were already highly developed arts. Indeed, one must wonder whether so unusual an art form as stained glass could ever have been born at all except in circumstances that were overwhelmingly favorable to it — a milieu in which the intrinsic qualities of the medium itself seemed almost to evoke what was most sought and demanded of the artistic image expressively, symbolically, architecturally. It was not until the mid- or late 15th century, when the conquest of natural appearance was already well under way, that the split between the aims of opaque painting and the means of the glasspainter began to be serious. But by that time even the aims of technology had begun to conspire against the art of stained glass; just as the production of larger, thinner and flatter sheets of glass was achieved at the cost of refractory richness, so the production of large sheets of paper now made it possible for the window designer to cartoon in his own studio. This can only have accelerated the growing estrangement of the window designer from the expressive resources of the medium.[3] By the second half of the 16th century the shift in visual sensibility was complete, and with that shift had come the kind of willful blindness to the non-malleable elements of the medium that we observed in the work of Romain Buron. How can we possibly account for such a development as this?

One can only assume that artists like Buron were attempting to carry over into stained glass a principle that, according to Geoffrey Scott (and the emphasis is his), was not only essential to Renaissance architecture but the mark of its genius: *"It realized that, for certain purposes in architecture, fact counted for everything, and that in certain others, appearances counted for everything. And it took advantage of this distinction to the full."* The tie-rod, for example, "the one constructional practice which distinguishes the Renaissance does but confirm the insignificant interest which construction, as such, possessed for the man of this period ... The eye was expected to disregard it as completely as it disregards the prop which in ancient sculpture supports a prancing horse."[4] However acceptable this practice may have been in architecture or sculpture — and even there it can hardly be counted as a virtue — it was a complete disaster in stained glass: a mechanical expediency too gross to be ignored, and for that reason the absolute enemy of pictorial illusion as an end in itself.

In fact, Scott's brilliant polemic against what he called the "romantic fallacy" — the displacement of formal by associative values in Gothic Revival architecture — provides us with a remarkably apt criticism of Renaissance stained glass. Echoing Scott, one can certainly declare that the primary values of stained glass, like those of humanist architecture, are sensuous and formal. Of all the arts stained glass is the one that most finds its natural expression in the immediate and the concrete — in the magnificent play of light upon a translucent material that is itself intrinsically interesting and that in the greatest cathedral windows is always rationally ordered. The first fallacy of the Renaissance, and the gravest, was to regard stained glass as an *illusionistic* art. This is not to suggest that illusionism has no place in it at all. "Every experience of art contains, or may contain, two elements, the one direct, the other indirect. The direct element includes our sensuous experience and simple perceptions of form: the immediate apprehension of the work of art in its visual or audible material, with whatever values may, by the laws of our nature, be inherently connected with that. Secondly, and beyond this, there are the associations which the work awakens in the mind — in our conscious reflections upon it, the significance we attach to it, the fancies it calls up, and which, in consequence, it is sometimes said to express. This is the indirect, or associative element.

"These two elements are present in nearly every aesthetic experience; but they may be very differently combined."[5] The primary appeal of illusionism is associative. This is not to say that illusionist art worthy of the name is entirely lacking in form; but its chief concern is with things and places envisioned — with what it effects to represent far more than with what it actually is. Nor is it to suggest "that we should *limit* our enjoyment of an art to that delight which it is the peculiar and special function of the art to provide. To sever our experience into such completely isolated departments is to impoverish it at every point. In the last resort, as in the first, we appreciate a work of art not by the single instrument of a specialized taste, but with our whole personality. Our experience is inevitably inclusive and synthetic. It extends far beyond the mere reaction to form. But its nucleus, at least, should be a right perception of that form, and of its aesthetic function."[6]

And in this right perception we should not lose sight of a problem that presents itself to the degree that this or any other art form becomes monumental: "Whatever surrounds us and contains our life, whatever is insistent and dominating; whatever permits us no escape . . . must be formal, coherent, and, in some sense, serene." Monumental stained glass, no less than architecture is such an art. "The different effects which art is able to produce, however various and incommensurable they may radically be, are commensurable at least in this: that each in some degree makes a demand on our *attention.* Some works of art affect us, as it were, by infiltration, and are calculated to produce an impression that is slow, pervasive, and profound. These seek neither to capture the attention nor to retain it; yet they satisfy it when it is given. Other works arrest us, and by a sharp attack upon the senses or the curiosity, insist upon our surrender. But since, as is well known, we cannot long react to a stimulus of this type, it is essential that the attention should, in these cases, be soon enough released. Otherwise, held captive and provoked, we are confronted with an insistent appeal which, since we can no longer respond to it, must become in time fatiguing or contemptible."[7]

Of all the visual arts there is probably none that can be so insistent and dominating as stained glass, or so inescapable as long as we are within its aura; yet it is to the windows of the 13th rather than the 16th century that we are drawn over and over again precisely because of their ultimate reserve, the perfect reciprocal adjustment of all their elements to one another. In short, the classical virtues par excellence. And it is Renaissance stained glass that, to the degree that it ventured into the realm of untrammeled illusion on a monumental scale, unwittingly became all of those things that, according to Scott, are anathema to humanist art: 'Overcharged with illustration and atrophied in its design, it finally ceases, in any aesthetic sense, to be significant at all.'[8]

Right: I. Ludwig Schaffrath: Cloister window, Aachen Cathedral, 1962-65.

III. The Sainte Chapelle, Paris, 1243-48.

Left: II. The west windows, Chartres Cathedral, the lancets c. 1155, the rose c. 1215.

IV. Peter Hemmel von Andlau: *St. Catherine*, Salzburg, c. 1480, Hessisches Landesmuseum, Darmstadt.

V. Georges Braque: *Tree of Jesse*, Varengeville (Seine-Maritime), 1961.

VI. Georg Meistermann: Choir windows, St. Mathew's Church, Sobernheim, 1964.

VII. Helmut Lander: Christ Church, Sennestadt, 1967-68.

Page 104: VIII. Robert Sowers: Residential window, Brooklyn, N.Y., 1980.

PART THREE: STAINED GLASS AND THE CONTEMPORARY ART WORLD

All the novelty-hunting that is later seen as faddishness, and not discovery, is assessed sooner and more truly by the mind ballasted with history.

— Jacques Barzun

IX *The Revival of Stained Glass*

Until the end of World War II, roughly half a century after the advent of modern art, stained glass suffered from a seemingly unshakeable incubus, traceable in large part to the circumstances under which this "lost art" had been rediscovered. Because the skills peculiar to it alone as a translucent art have no real counterpart in any other medium, they were to all intents and purposes literally lost — abandoned as artistically irrelevant during the course of the 17th and 18th centuries. Hence we can see how nearly inevitable it was that their rediscovery should have come about as it did: as part and parcel of an aesthetically reactionary movement like the Gothic Revival. Indeed, we may doubt whether this extremely elusive and mutually interrelated body of artistic, architectural and technical skills could ever have been rediscovered at all had the partisans of that movement been any less avid in their almost slavish effort to duplicate the effects of the Gothic. In any case, it is to the impetus of the Gothic Revival that we are finally indebted not only for the revival of the craft — an altogether remarkable achievement — but for the problem that was to plague the art for nearly a century thereafter: how to escape from the debilitating confines of pseudo-medievalism? How to enlist its unrivalled resources of color and luminosity in the service of a genuinely contemporary vision? By and large, those who had become involved in the revival of stained glass had neither the talent nor the temperament to venture beyond the sheltering authority of the past, while those who might well have done so, lacked the requisite skills.

Thus for nearly that whole period almost every durable milestone in the rivival of this art was the work of some gifted interloper — someone who came to it neither from the stained-glass studios nor from the world of painting. The first authoritative study of glasspainting techniques was written by the English lawyer to whom we have already referred, Charles Winston;[1] Viollet-le-Duc was an architect and civil servant; the first really important stained glass windows were the product of a unique collaboration between the English designer and social reformer William Morris and the pre-Raphaelite painter Sir Edward Burne-Jones, that began c. 1860.[2] As Herbert Read tells us, Morris "realized that a good craftsman was not necessarily a great artist. Such, he might have said to himself, was the whole difference between himself and his friend, Burne-Jones. He therefore determined to go for his designs to the best artist he knew of — and this was Burne-Jones; he then translated these designs himself into the appropriate technical medium ... In this manner two essentials were secured: a design of imaginative worth free from the cramping influence (and mere imaginative insufficiency) of the craftsman, and a technical execution of this design free from the craft amateurishness of the imaginative artist." Of Morris's contribution to the windows that resulted from this collaboration Read says: "His selection and disposition of colours is admirable, and he was not afraid of using new colours to achieve effects unknown to previous ages. In the use of leads to emphasize design he is masterly, and we must go back again to the 13th century for an adequate comparison."[3]

On the basis of this achievement Read concluded that "the principles which William Morris established and followed give us an adequate criterion for the criticism of modern stained glass"; but he felt constrained to add: "It is sad to confess how little these principles have been followed in England itself. There is no longer any vital contact between the glass-painters and the significant artists of the day. And in all directions there is a relapse into a servile and lifeless imitation of medieval mannerisms." However, he continued, "these principles are not altogether dead: they have merely migrated, and on the continent, especially in Germany, there is a school of glass-painting which is not only modern in intention, but is inspired by all that is vital and significant in modern art . . . we have on the one hand the profoundly moving and sincere work of Jan Thorn-Prikker, who has given to the symbols and images of Christianity a new intensity and realism for which there is no parallel this side of the Renaissance; and on the other hand we have the abstract designs of Karl Schmidt-Rottluff and again of Thorn-Prikker which seem to open up infinite possibilities for this art of pure colour and light."[4]

When we consider that Mr. Read's book was published in 1926, we realize how remarkably astute these comments were; Thorn Prikker was destined to become the father of the present German school of stained glass. Yet we have had ample occasion since then to learn that the "vital contact" of which Read speaks, and which is so evident in this new school, is not established simply by bringing the best artists and craftsmen together. Indeed, this may be one of the most enduring lessons to be learned from the great collaborative efforts that were made in France shortly after World War II, as remarkable as some of them were. For the extraordinary prestige of the artists — combined in some cases with their advanced age and ill health — seems often to have had the paradoxical effect of isolating them from just those aspects of the art that one might otherwise have expected them to exploit.

Typical of this isolation was the relationship between Matisse, who was bedridden in the south of France, and Paul Bony, who executed the windows for the Vence chapel in Paris. Because Matisse had chosen an extremely brilliant yellow glass for them, Bony sought the artist's permission to counter its inevitable halation into the adjacent, much darker greens and blues by shrinking the contours of all the yellow shapes in the design by half the thickness of a leadline; but Matisse's zealously protective intermediaries would hear of no such tampering with the master's handiwork. So Bony was forced, much against his better judgment, to follow the artist's cartoons literally and with the predictable result: when Matisse saw the completed windows he found the yellow too dominant, and they had to be made all over again. It is not hard to

imagine this great artist under more favorable circumstances seizing upon the
unusual volatility of the colors in stained glass to create one prodigious harmony
after another. As it is, the Vence windows, magnificently, intuitively right
though they are, are less like the late work of the greatest colorist of our time
than the first notable achievement of a very promising young stained-glass
artist — which is what Matisse at the age of eighty was.

The windows that Braque designed for his local church in Varengeville are
equally interesting because they enable us to see how this artist might have
developed after a rather unpromising start into a superb glasspainter. The
St. Dominic window and its two flanking ornamental lights, completed in 1954,
are almost totally lacking in the rich material subtleties that this artist's name
automatically calls to mind. One gets the impression that he must have been
almost over-intimidated by the bold-line, brilliant-color rudiments of the medi-

um. Seven years later, however, when Braque returned to stained glass to design a *Jesse Tree* for the same church the result, illustrated on page 101, was a masterful creation.

Elsewhere, however, one finds really drastic shortcomings. In Assy, for example, Bony was employed to do nothing more nor less than duplicate, by whatever technical means he could contrive, a series of Rouault paintings that the sponsors of the church had found suitable in subject matter and which the artist had lent for this purpose. Here, in other words, was the "servile and lifeless imitation" not of another period style but of a whole repertoire of modern painterly effects that in stained glass count for almost nothing. *This is the craft tyrannized by art.* The more recent windows of Chagall are at least more authentic in this respect. From start to finish they are intended to be stained glass and they are painted by the artist himself; but in them we find ourselves confronted with an aggressive disarray of leadlines and uncertain armature divisions that appear to be the uncritically accepted contribution of Chagall's craftsman-collaborators at the Atelier Jacques Simon.[5] *This is art mindlessly encumbered by the craft.*

In the case of such "painterly" painters as Chagall, however, there is often still another problem that may be illustrated with one of this artist's works: *Hammarskjold Memorial* at the United Nations. As John Canaday was quick to point out, this work "is poorly related to its architectural setting and, as an extremely personal expression, is also out of key with the monumentality that stained glass as an adjunct to architecture must have ... The artist has made strenuous objections to the setting of the memorial (again avoiding the word window), and his objections are valid, although a conter-objection could be that he should have taken the setting into consideration in creating the design. The light at either side is too bright, reducing the window's brilliance. On a sunlit afternoon it bleaches out. The floor, of black and white squares measuring about three feet, is not only too powerful for the small, broken forms of the stained glass but is also unrelated to the dimensions of the iron grid that serves as a framework, giving the impression that the memorial is placed where it is for temporary exhibition."[6] In other words, it fails to establish any formal relationship with its setting at all, let alone the kind one expects from a memorial. *This is architecture abused and meaning confounded.*

What Herbert Read simply took for granted in the case of William Morris and Burne-Jones — the rare meeting of minds, dating all the way back to their student days at Oxford; their exactly complementary skills; and their sustained collaboration over a period of some three decades — helps us to understand how these men were able to accomplish what they did. Between them they were able to function as *one mind,* one complete master of this art, who could therefore confidently delegate the cutting, firing and glazing of their windows to others in such a manner that the results would not get out of hand. The lesson is plain. Only to the extent that the artist is himself a master of the craft, i.e., only to the extent that he is able to visualize and control everything that will in any way affect the final appearance of his stained-glass window in its intended setting, can he hope to create a work

of art — or will the work created be truly his own. This is to claim no more for stained glass than one would claim for any other complex art form: that it cannot be sustained, let alone advanced, by the occasional efforts, however inspired, of artists whose primary commitment is to some other medium.

Left: 62. Georges Rouault: *Christ Scourged*, oil on paper, 1939; and 63. the window in Assy.

To be sure, the first recognizably modern windows were the work of such architects as Gaudí, Mackintosh and Wright — but they do not pretend to be anything more than ornament. And when finally we come to Matisse and Léger we may note, without detracting from their achievement in the least, that at the time they created their stained-glass windows each of these artists happened to be working in a manner that quite by chance lent itself rather directly to translation into stained glass. In other words, prior to the advent of the present German school of stained glass the revival of the art had consisted of little more than the brilliant but infrequent and generally isolated efforts of those for whom stained glass was but one interest among many. The wonder, therefore, is not that this revival had been such a long drawn-out and tenuous affair but that it had accomplished as much as it had.

Because the revival of stained glass has been so frequently and ineffectually proclaimed, let us note first of all how radically the present German school of stained glass differs from anything that we have seen before. Assy, Coventry and the Jerusalem windows of Chagall were all the focus of some particular cultural bootstrap operation with social and political implications that went quite beyond any concern with stained glass, as such, and hence were celebrated out of all proportion to their artistic merit. The German works illustrated on these pages are but a fair sampling of a widespread and deep-rooted development *in stained glass,* until recently almost completely unknown outside of Germany, and only very modestly publicized there. And whereas we have come to expect the latest "new look" in stained glass to consist of little more than a congeries of half-assimilated hand-me-downs from painting, or some gimmicky new technique, this work is rooted in the oldest and simplest elements of the craft. Yet such technical innovations as one does see, in Ludwig Schaffrath's prism windows, for example, or Wilhelm Buschulte's cut-steel-plate and slab-glass windows, are brilliantly conceived. The latter, in the charming eight-hundred-year-old Church of St. Clemens in Drolshagen, perform the seemingly impossible feat of looking completely contemporary and at the same time almost more Romanesque than Romanesque. And finally, whereas the stained-glass windows of Rouault, Villon and Chagall, Piper, Rattner and Gottlieb have always seemed either labored or uncertain in scale, the relation between these works and their architectural settings seems nearly always to be both right and reciprocal. The architects no less than the artists have learned how to think authentically in terms of this very architectural medium, and thus to conceive new and daring ways to utilize it. Notable among such works is the new Christ Church in Sennestadt (pages 103,119), in which the architect Dieter Oesterlen and artist Helmut Lander have created a vast fenestration of alternating slab-glass and clear plate-glass elements that draw the atmosphere of the surrounding glade of trees into the church itself.

What we have here, in short, is nothing less than the first full-fledged *school*

Left: 64. Marc Chagall: *Dag Hammarskjöld Memorial*, United Nations Secretariat, New York, N.Y., 1964.

of stained glass since the Middle Ages — the first cumulative development, over a period of some three generations, of an original approach to this art, authentically grounded in and exploiting to an unprecedented degree certain of its unique potentialities as a medium. And here also we find the first truly productive division of labor and responsibilities — the first arrangement for commissioning, designing and executing stained-glass windows that can be justified by its results — since the decline of the medieval guilds. To examine this achievement is therefore to discover, far more concretely than ever before, what the revival of stained glass actually entails.

The most destinctive achievement of the German school is quite unlike anything that any sequence of unrelated creations, or even individual careers, could ever have produced. It is the intensive refinement, into what might be called a kind of graphic "logic," of the leadline (or concrete infilling) by means of which the stained-glass window is typically assembled. This structurally necessary element has been transformed into a major expressive device that, most notably in the work of Ludwig Schaffrath,[7] approaches a consummate elegance. Here we are on ground that was never more than tentatively explored in the 12th and 13th centuries, and it is now being exploited with great individual distinction by several artists.

Another important characteristic of this new work is its singular combination of the muralesque and the expressionistic — a combination of qualities that has not been seen in so pure a form, in Western art at any rate, since the Romanesque. It is important here to distinguish between the muralesque and what is sometimes referred to as "architectonic" composition in painting. Poussin and Cézanne are masters of architectonic composition but neither is particularly muralesque. Neither is so literally "of the wall" that his smallest drawing can be enlarged a hundredfold, like a 12th-century illumination, without serious loss of effect. Nor were the great ceiling painters from Guido Reni to Tiepolo so much "of" as "beyond" the wall, i.e., brilliantly and systematically *anti*-muralesque — which was absolutely right for the architecture of their time. But not only was the Romanesque an art of the wall; the agitated rhythms, bold distortions and frequently strange color harmonies of much Romanesque art make it seem formally akin to modern expressionistic painting. This particular combination of qualities always bespeaks a disciplined ardor, whether in the late archaic Greek, in Romanesque, Japanese or pre-Columbian art, and it is testimony to the high seriousness of these German stained-glass artists that their work has begun to evoke it again.

The working relationship between these artists and the stained-glass studios can be defined in a sentence. The artist is directly commissioned to conceive and himself execute or otherwise control the execution of all aspects of the work that will in any way affect its final appearance as a work of art. Those who are commissioned to assist the artist are commissioned to do no more — and no less — than to assist him in the realization of a work that will not only be faithful to his conception but be a physical creation of the finest possible workmanship. In short, this new relationship presupposes the mastery of this demanding medium that, as we have already seen, was so difficult

Right: 65. Ludwig Schaffrath: St. Michael's Church, Schweinfurt, 1967-68.

67. Ludwig Schaffrath: Christi-Geburt Parish Church, Cologne-Mengenich, 1971.

Left: 66. Medallion window, exterior, Canterbury Cathedral, c. 1200.

69. Johannes Schreiter: St. Margaret's Church, Burgstadt-on-the-Main, 1960.

Left: 68. Jochem Poensgen: New Catholic Church, Bad Honnef-Selhof, 1968.

Page 118: 70. Ewald Mataré: Rathaus, Aachen, 1962.

Page 119: 71. Helmut Lander: Christ Church, Sennestadt, 1967-68; detail.

72. and 73. Johan Thorn Prikker: Retrospective exhibition, Kaiser Wilhelm Museum, Krefeld, 1932.

if not pointless for the artist to acquire so long as stained glass was little more than a kept technique in the hands of the revivalists. On the evidence of the works shown here he has now clearly acquired that mastery, and the studios function primarily as ateliers for the execution of his works. Here then, if anywhere, we see an end to the fatal dichotomy that has frustrated the revival of a great and glorious art for more than a century: taste and talent on the one hand, but with insufficient grounding in the essentials of the craft; ample skills and facilities on the other, all devoted to doing a brisk know-nothing trade in sub-Camp religious candy.

Thus the sterile conflict between the stained-glass studios and the artist is finally resolved, and in exactly the same simple, logical way that it has always been resolved between the sculptor and foundry; tapestry designer and weaver; architect, contractor and building trades; composer, conductor and orchestra; choreographer and dancers; or the creator of anything else in which some division of labor is a practical necessity. There really is nothing very mysterious about it at all. But how, it may be asked, are we to account for such a development in Germany and Germany alone? This much can be said with at least some degree of assurance, that only in Germany did all of the following conditions exist after World War II: the massive opportunity created by the devastation of the war, both for the restoration of old and the creation of a new public architecture; a generally enlightened patronage; a long and indigenous tradition of architectural arts and crafts that had never been wholly subordinated to the fine arts; and the seminal pre-war example set by Johan Thorn Prikker[8] and such architects as Rudolf Schwarz and Dominikus Bohm. Perhaps all of these conditions (or their equivalent elsewhere, such as the massive postwar building boom in the United States) must be considered indispensable for the birth of a full-fledged school of stained glass. Obviously, where one or more of these conditions did *not* exist — in France, England, Switzerland or the United States — there has been no comparable development, only intimations of it, as the brief sampling of American works on pages 155-163 attempts to suggest.

In sum, the German achievement has been to return to the most basic elements of stained glass — glass, lead and light — and to exploit them directly, imaginatively and singlemindedly, on a vast scale and without stint, for more than a quarter of a century. And thanks to the collaboration of a body of singularly imaginative architects, from Schwarz and Bohm to Dieter Oesterlen and Hans Schädel, they have exploited the contemporary possibilities of fenestration with a daring that has no precedent since the Gothic era. Finally emancipated from the special concerns of easel painting and conceived as a bona fide art form in its own right, contemporary German stained glass is ultimately beholden to nothing but its own standards of excellence. Thus here, if anywhere, the revival of stained glass has been transformed into an impressive reality.

But the balance of forces that produces an achievement of this kind can seldom be long sustained. Precisely because it is so compelling, and in the last analysis so communal, it is bound sooner or later to create a dilemma

Right: 74. Georg Meistermann: *Pascal* window, Sepulchur, Wurzburg Cathedral, 1957.

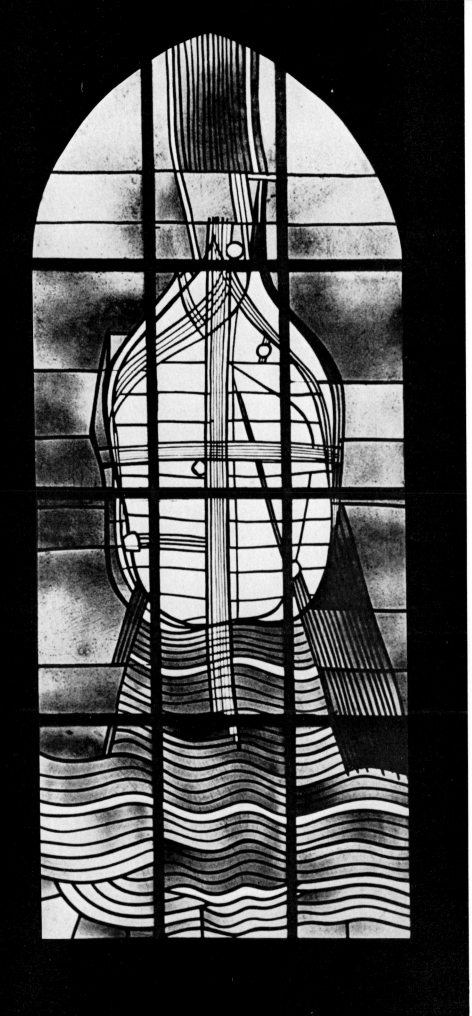

76. Georg Meistermann: St. Mary's Church, Cologne-Kalk, 1965.

Left: 75. Georg Meistermann: Choir windows, St. Moritz, Augsburg.

Page 126: 77. Maria Katzgrau: Choir windows, St. Anna, Duisberg.

Page 127: 78. Maria Katzgrau: Choir window, Liebfrau Kloster, Eschweiler, 1968.

Page 128: 79. Maria Katzgrau: St. Elizabeth's Church, Aachen, 1979.

Page 129: 80. Maria Katzgrau: St. Bonifatius, Aachen-Forst.

Page 130: 81. Wilhelm Buschulte: St. Foillan, Aachen, 1960.

Page 131: 82. Wilhelm Buschulte: Essen Cathedral, 1965.

Page 132: 83. Wilhelm Buschulte: St. Paul's Church, Lövenich, 1973.

Page 133: 84. Wilhelm Buschulte: St. Pius, Münster.

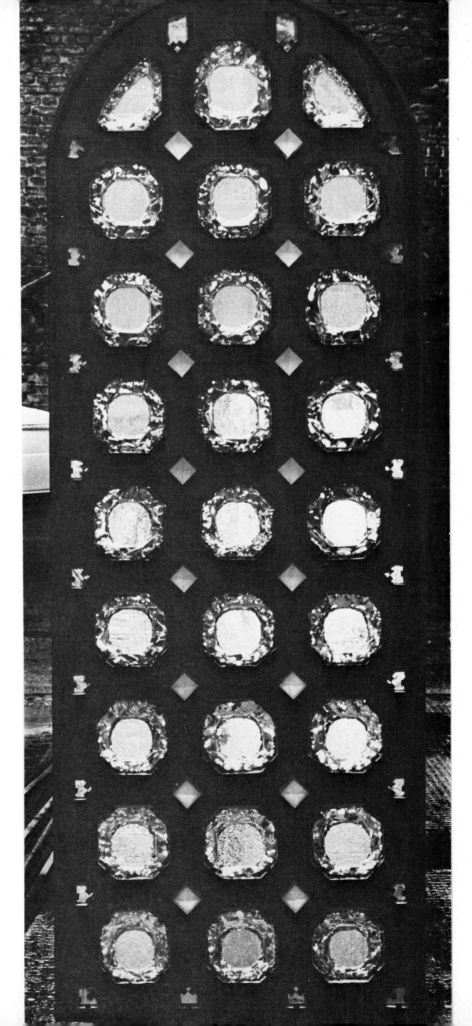

85. Wilhelm Buschulte: Ratzeburg Cathedral, 1969.

Right: 86. Wilhelm Buschulte: Choir windows, Church of Sts. Peter and Paul, Wegburg.

Page 136: 87. Jochem Poensgen: Augustinian Museum, Frieburg, 1979.

Page 137: 88. Hubert Spierling: Choir window, Maria Laach.

Pages 138 and 139: 89. and 90. Johannes Schreiter: Hiigh School Auditorium, Bonn-Tannenbusch, 1966.

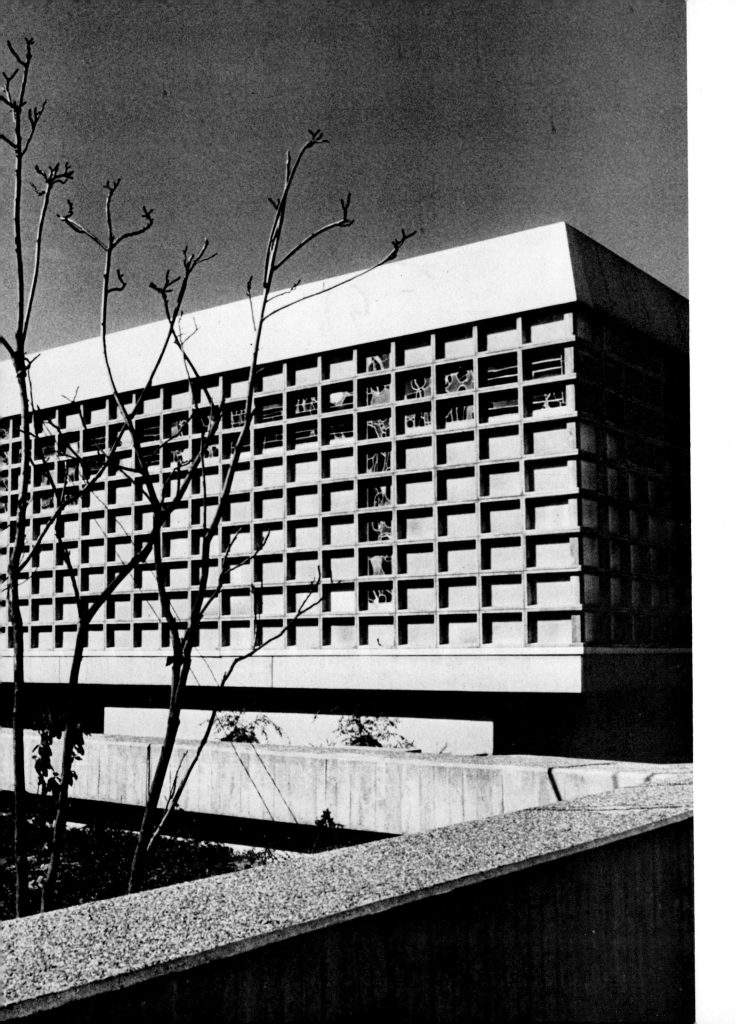

91. and 92. Johannes Schreiter: Cloister Chapel, Order of St. John, Leutesdorf-on-the-
Rhine, 1966.

93. Johannes Schreiter: St. John's Church, Bremerhaven, 1966.

Right: 94. Johannes Schreiter: Catholic Church, Werneck, 1968.

Pages 144 and 145: 95. and 96. Johannes Schreiter: St. Mary's Church, Dortmund, 1972.

Pages 148 and 149: 99. and 100. Ludwig
Schaffrath: St. Pankratius, Rurdorf,
1967.

98. Ludwig Schaffrath: Maria Heimsu-
chung, Alsdorf-Schaufenberg.

Left: 97. Ludwig Schaffrath: St. Peter's
Church, Birkesdorf, 1964.

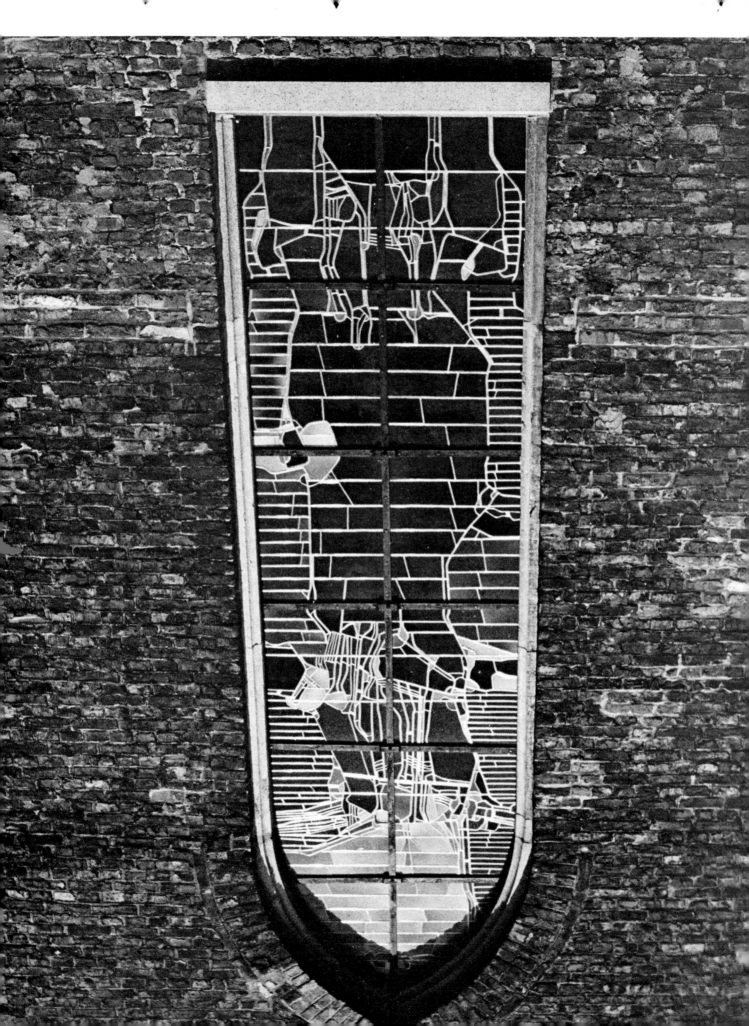

Pages 152 and 153: 103. and 104. Ludwig Schaffrath: St. Josef's Church, Aachen, 1971-73.

Right: 102. Ludwig Schaffrath: St. Peter's Church, Merken.

101. Ludwig Schaffrath: Priesterhaus, Maria-Rast, Aachen, 1967.

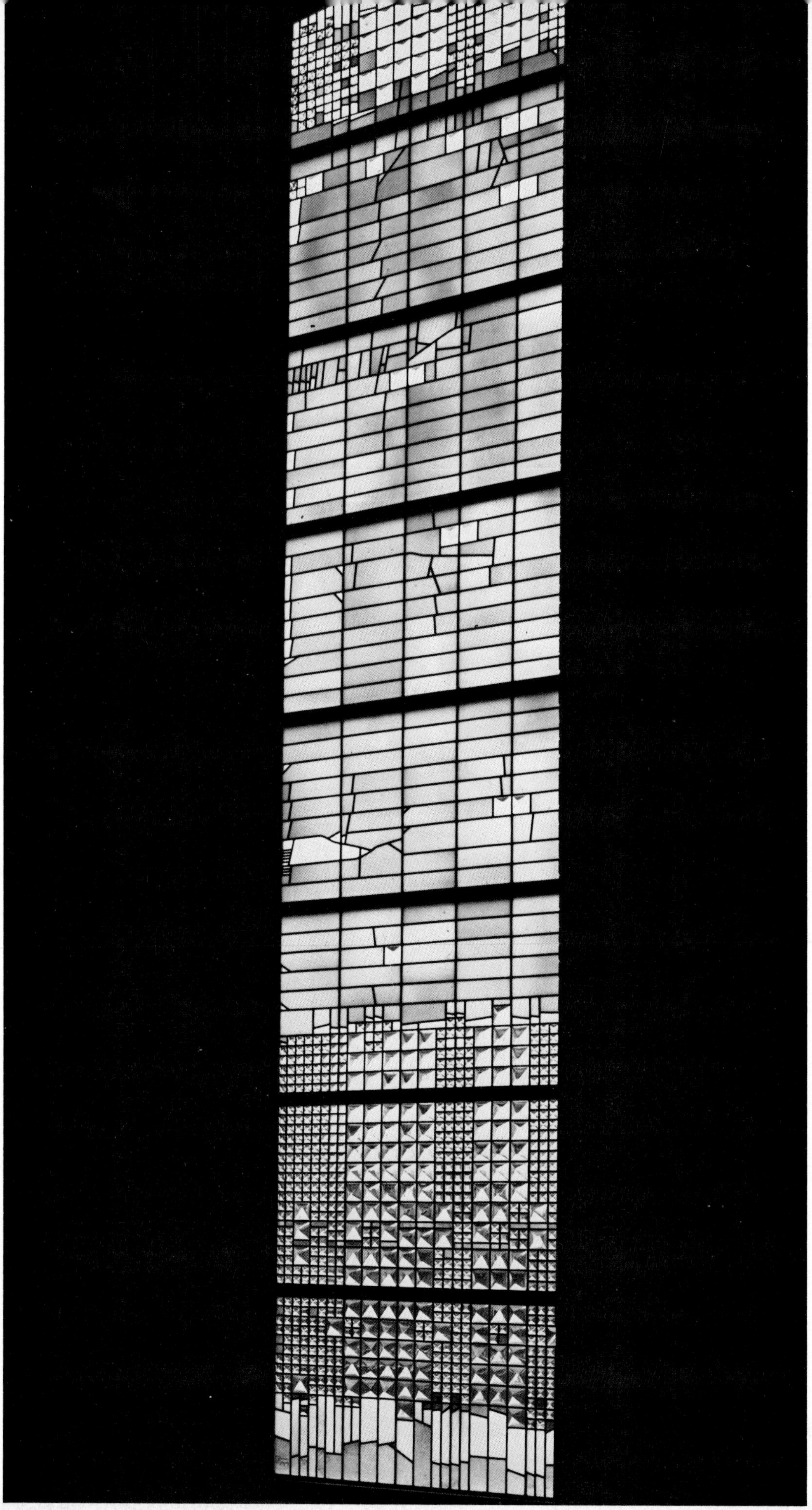

105. Ludwig Schaffrath: St. Mary's Church, Bad Zwischenahn, 1970.

Right: 106. Ray King: Glass element for One Jericho Plaza, Jericho, N.Y., 1978.

Page 156: 107. Ed Carpenter: Oregon School of Arts and Crafts, Portland, 1979.

Page 157: 108. Julia Wirick Kingsley: Private residence, Louisville, Ky., 1980.

Page 158: 109. David Wilson: Church of St. Thomas More, Cherry Hill, N.J., 1979.

Page 159: 110. Kenneth vonRoenn: Clyde's Restaurant, Vienna, Va., 1979-80.

Page 160: 111. Marni Bakst: Lasser *Window I*, Hackettstown, N.J., 1978.

Page 161: 112. Robert Pinart: Window for the Gordon Cuyler residence, New York.

for the artist who must follow in its wake. To acknowledge the authority of a "classic" solution is to risk being overwhelmed by it — the invariable fate of all *classicisms*. The problem is at least as old as the Hellenistic reaction against Periclean art in the 4th century B.C., and so are the basic strategies for challenging the authority of a classical style: virtuosity, mannerism, parody, the systematic inversion of values. That some of the Germans should have begun to challenge the premises of their own work after such a long period of remarkably self-assured creation can only be regarded as an index of their continuing artistic probity. But with that observation we must be content for the present to leave them. To attempt anything more would be both premature and speculative, a journalistic distraction from the stated aims of this book.

There is another current development, however, that we cannot decently ignore since it calls into question one of the chief premises of our analysis thus far. The vital link between stained glass and architecture — the one thing that Renaissance stained glass never explicitly challenged even in its bravura miniaturist phase — recently has been challenged, especially in the United States, through the development of a mode of stained-glass design that is essentially painterly, technically innovative, and avowedly non-architectural. The independently created stained-glass panel is conceived of as an autonomous museum or gallery object. Here again, any attempt to appraise this development in detail would be premature; but the concept of autonomy itself is so beguiling, and the problems it poses for the art of stained glass are so fundamental, that it deserves a chapter of its own.

Right: 113. Peter Mollica: Architect's conference room, Marquis Associates, San Francisco.

According to *Webster's Third International Dictionary*, autonomy is a political and moral concept, pure and simple: "the quality of being independent, free, and self-directing," and it is only by a kind of loose analogy that the term has found its way into talk about the visual arts. Like so many honorific terms of this kind it *seems* to make sense until its credentials are really examined, whereupon its meaning turns out to be anything but clear. What then of visual autonomy? In what sense or to what degree are visual forms as we actually perceive them autonomous — truly "independent, free, and self-directing"?

Let us attempt to see.

Paradoxically, the first thing that one discovers when one attempts to measure the autonomy of a simple form, such as the circle in the accompanying series of diagrams, is that it clearly is due less to any superior internal organization, complexity, or intrinsic interest — the most commonly assumed qualities of visual autonomy — than to its relation to its background. Thus, when the blank circle in A is filled in with black, increasing its contrast with its background as in B, its autonomy is greatly increased; but when the background is also filled in as in C, that increase is largely negated. Similarly, the autonomy of the blank circle can be increased by filling in its background alone, as in D. And here one is reminded of the oculus in the dome of the Pantheon, illustrated on page 31, which as we have already seen is one of the most commanding, or autonomous, forms in the history of architecture even though it is quite literally a void. Finally, if we think of our circle as though it were indeed transparent like the oculus of the Pantheon, we realize that it absolutely requires some powerful framing element, such as the architectural framing of a window automatically provides, to prevent it from merging with its background as it threatens to do in E. Admittedly, the circle is no work of art, yet the implications of these diagrams are too clear-cut to be ignored: *that visual autonomy, far from being an absolute condition, is always highly relative; that it may quite as easily be reinforced by architecture; and that it is fundamentally incompatible with transparency, which is to say, with one of the most distinctive qualities of stained glass.*

But to come to our subject more directly; even in the museum visual autonomy, whatever else it may be, is no index of quality. A line of Kufic script on a pottery shard may well exhibit more expressive force than a whole room full of 19th-century salon paintings. There also, the picture frame and the pedestal, the classical insignia of the fine arts and an important instrument of their autonomy, will be employed to puff up routine and pretentious works

115. Entrance to the Palazzo Vecchio, Florence.

114. The autonomy of a circle.

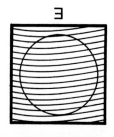

E

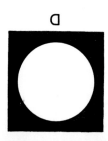

D

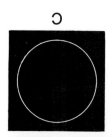

C

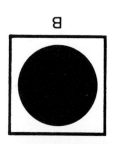

B

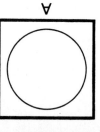

A

no less than genuine works of art. And when frames and pedestals are virtually eliminated as they are in the case of much contemporary work, the autonomy of that work may become problematical — is sometimes deliberately made so for a variety of "conceptual" reasons that are also more ideological than visual. But in fact, the autonomy of *any* new creation — genuinely new even to the artist who has made it, and however good it may eventually be considered to be — is likely to be more than a little problematical. As I have noted elsewhere, "A painting that is framed no longer means the same thing that it meant on the easel; the same thing hanging on the wall that it means leaning against a wall; not the same thing in a one-man show that it means in a group show or may later mean in a retrospective; nor the same thing on one wall rather than another wall in any given show; nor the same as any of these things on the walls of a collector's living room, dining room, bedroom, cocktail bar, yacht, picture gallery or private chapel, or the walls of any public place."[1]

Lest our analysis may seem to have strayed too far from the art of stained glass, let us bring it back home. First of all, we may note that a great many stained-glass artists, from Ludwig Schaffrath to Paul Marioni, have created both uncommissioned panels and architectural windows without significantly altering either the style or complexity of their work. Secondly, that architectural windows or parts of them have often been exhibited as autonomous works and independently created panels sometimes incorporated into architecture. And finally, that certain recent works like Ray King's in One Jericho Plaza (p. 155) defy classification either way. As a touchstone for either quality or originality the concept of autonomy simply dissolves between our fingers. It is only when the new panelists begin to refer to everyone else as "traditionalists"[2] that one begins to get the point: "Autonomy" is less an artistic concept than a battle cry — the latest attempt to redefine the terms of the New. Once this is understood it becomes possible to talk about these recent uncommissioned panels with at least some degree of objectivity.

Here again as in the case of Renaissance stained glass, we can ask what the stained-glass artist sacrifices and what he gains when he seeks to transform the expressive character of the medium itself. To begin with the gains, he gains a significant freedom not only from the traditional function of the stained-glass window but from the restrictions of budgets, deadlines and orthodox techniques. He is free to do whatever his materials and imagination permit. Here, for example, is Paul Marioni's description of how one of his early panels evolved: "OPEN HEART SURGERY — I have seen pictures of very old cars with the inner tubes creeping out around the rim of the tire and this gave me the idea for a chest of drawers with an inner tube coming out of the drawer. It was a great opportunity to break out of the square or rectangle shape that everybody seems stuck with. By making the drawer open it looks as though it is three-dimensional. I used a single sheet of clear reamy antique for the chest of drawers, cutting it in a way similar to a matched wood veneer. The side of the drawer is clear seedy antique, which seems to me what a cross section of the clear reamy would look like — if that were possible. The

inner tube is made from a very unusual red opaque glass that comes in a pizza-like round shape and looks like a piece of raw liver — shiny, dark red. The inner tube reminded me of a heart when it was finished, so I called the window OPEN HEART SURGERY. I wanted to mount clear glass drawer pulls like the ones on my living room bookcases. Since I live in an old house, however, I discovered that I couldn't get that kind anymore. So finally I took the ones off the bookcases to use in this window."[3]

Whatever else one may say, this is authentic thinking in terms of *glass* — of the physical character and substance of the medium itself — and works like this are immeasurably more challenging, more interesting and above all more fun than the glossy ineptitudes of a Piper or Chagall. In such canny

116. Paul Marioni: *Open Heart Surgery*.

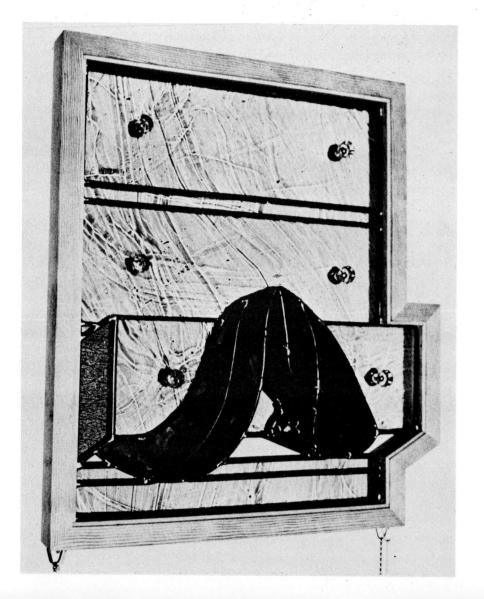

stripping down and overloading of the medium the best of these new artists are not only performing an extremely valuable critical function; in the process they are making stained glass accessible to a far wider and more varied public than it ever enjoyed before. So much to the good. But inescapably these gains are purchased at a price.

First of all, there is no getting away from the fact that the architectural setting normally presents the stained-glass artist with a whole range of specific and thus readily exploitable natural-light conditions that to a very large extent are simply unavailable to the maker of autonomous panels, or that he cannot count on being available for his work once it leaves his hands. "Ultimately, it is the delicate interplay of light, glass and lead — the substance of stained glass to which we respond," says Robert Kehlmann in introducing the recent exhibition of "New Stained Glass" at the Museum of Contemporary Crafts.[4] Exactly so; and it is hard to see how this delicate interplay, which we have attempted to describe in earlier chapters, can be either left to chance or contrived non-architecturally.

Second, if it is to be seen at all the independently conceived panel must obviously be displayed *somewhere*. And if only by default that somewhere is more than likely to be a gallery, whose white walls and artificial lighting can be counted upon to obliterate many of the most singular refractory qualities of stained glass. Here again, I must quote Robert Kehlmann, because of all the new panelists he has most clearly confronted this difficulty and sought to deal with it in his own work: "By keeping my compositions subdued I try not to exploit people's instinctive attraction to colored light. My pieces are not 'colorful' in the Gothic and Tiffany stained glass window traditions that stress strong color contrasts. Rather, activity of brightness and color are subordinated to activity of form and line ... Since I am interested in the two-dimensional surface I work exclusively with translucent glass which stops the eye at the surface of each panel. The surface of my compositions are central to their effect since the viewer stands directly in front of them. The relief of lead and glass, the different textures, assume a visual and tactile importance they cannot have in a window located far from the viewer's reach ... Many of my works are placed in stands which permit for simple display. The viewer can walk around a stand and see the work as a whole. This accents the 'ob-jectness' of each piece."[5] Pursuing the implications of this approach to its logical conclusion Kehlmann calls his compositions "lead and glass drawings" because they have a closer relationship to drawings than to stained glass." That such works capture the look of a certain kind of "automatic" drawing, especially in photographs, cannot be denied; but this is to overlook both the radical differences in technique and spontaneity, and the obvious sculptural concerns voiced by Kehlmann in his own statement. One can only wish him well, for whatever these works are called he has put himself in a most unenviable position: peripheral to at least three well defined arts yet almost certain to be judged by the criteria of all three.

Rather than attempt to compete with gallery art on such unequal terms the panelmaker may adopt the strategies of Dada and Surrealism, Funk and

117. Robert Kehlmann: "Lead and Glass Drawings," William Sawyer Gallery, San Francisco, 1978.

Pop Art, as many of them already have[6] — the bland and the mock-serious, the obsessive and the lowbrow, the gadgetry and the erotic — to run full tilt against the still popular conception of stained glass as a pious Victorian confection. But by doing so he places himself in an even more tenuous position: dependent for the shock value of his work upon the mere novelty of its *being* stained glass. Or finally, confronted with all of the more intractible elements of the medium itself, which become increasingly limiting and obtrusive the more stained glass is reduced in scale, he may resort to feats of technical legerdemain, not unlike those employed by the tour-de-force miniaturists of the 16th and 17th centuries (pages 89 and 90). But the more painstaking and time-consuming these become the more pressing must become the question, to others if not to himself: *Why stained glass at all?*

To all of this there is an obvious, attractive, and yet not wholly satisfactory answer. Confronted with an architecture whose leading practitioners were plainly uncomfortable not just with stained glass but with all of the allied arts — an architecture that proclaimed its own narrowly formalistic autonomy with an almost Puritanical zeal — these panel makers, joined in some cases by architectural artists of long standing, really had little choice but to attempt to go it alone. Hence the vitality, the fantasy and the ingenuity of the best of this work is not only real, it has been created against all odds. Undoubtedly, this is true. But we are still left with the problems I have enumerated; they too are very real; to the extent that they are inherent in the nature of the medium they will not go away. And we are left with the question with which we began: How to account for the almost charismatic attraction of visual auton-omy — a phenomenon that according to our analysis can scarcely be said to exist?

Perhaps the answer lies so close at hand that we have overlooked it altogether. For it is a fact that photographs, in magazines, in books like this one, but above all in the form of color slides projected on a screen, tend to have an aggrandizing effect on works of art — most particularly small works, or details excerpted from larger ones. Plucked out of context and projected on the screen, a figure that one might never notice in Chartres suddenly acquires a dramatic monumentality, a visual impact that is out of all proportion to its effect in the actual window. Yet there can be little doubt that we tend to read such *purely photographic aggrandizement back into the thing itself.* Similarly, the photograph of a stained-glass panel taken under ideal light conditions and cropped so that nothing else shows *is visually autonomous* in a variety of ways that the work itself can never be; and this too undoubtedly gets read back into it. If that is the case, then the question we ought to be asking is, which is actually function-ing as the governing norm, the stained glass itself or its photographic image? How, through the agency of the camera, do we affect our perception of this art in the very act of trying to study and document it? This is the question that we must now consider.

Left: 118. Harriet Hyams: *Glas Architektur I.*

XI Stained-Glass Windows in the "Museum Without Walls"

For the last hundred years (if we except the activities of specialists) art history has been the history of that which can be photographed. —André Malraux

Malraux dreams, without doubt, of being the Lawrence of archeology.

—Georges Duthuit

As we have already seen, the stained-glass window is so much a creature of light that it can rarely meet the viewer halfway in a museum or gallery without being radically transformed in the process. How it is visually documented and presented to the viewer on the printed page ought therefore, to be a matter of more than academic interest, or the kind of academic interest that it has generated thus far, beginning with the critical reception to André Malraux's "Museum Without Walls."[1]

In that work Malraux sets the stage for his radical reinterpretation of art by reminding us how recent historically and atypical culturally are our great museums *with* walls, and how drastically they in their turn had changed the terms in which art was conceived: "So vital is the part played by the art museum in our approach to works of art today that we find it difficult to realize that no museums exist, none has ever existed, in lands where the civilization of modern Europe is, or was, unknown; and that, even amongst us, they have existed for barely two hundred years. They bulked so large in the nineteenth century and are so much a part of our lives today that we forget they have imposed on the spectator a wholly new attitude towards the work of art. For they have tended to estrange the works they bring together from their original functions and to transform even portraits into 'pictures.'" He then goes on to show us how the camera is now revolutionizing this museum-bred conception of art. Because it nullifies differences of location photography is bringing together on the printed page the most widely dispersed creations for direct one-to-one comparison; because it tends to minimize differences of material and size, it is revealing to us many hitherto unsuspected stylistic affinities between otherwise diverse creations: "In our Museum Without Walls picture, fresco, miniature and stained-glass window seem of one and the same family. For all alike — miniatures, frescoes, stained glass, tapestries, Scythian plaques, pictures, Greek vase paintings, 'details' and even statuary — have become 'collotypes.' In the process they have lost their properties as *objects*; but, by the same token, they have gained something: the utmost significance as to style that they can possibly acquire." Thus, "alongside the museum a new field

of art experience, vaster than any so far known, is now, thanks to reproductions, being opened up. And in this new domain — which is growing more and more intellectualized as our stocktaking and its diffusion proceeds and methods of reproduction come nearer to fidelity — is for the first time the common heritage of all mankind."[2]

That the photograph *can* do the things Malraux says it can do he proves with his own book, which is itself a brilliant if somewhat vertiginous rollercoaster ride through our visual heritage. Without question the camera can isolate and bring to our attention all sorts of unexpected, purely visual similarities between the most diverse creations — some of which are as meretricious as others are significant; but *must* the camera inevitably convert all works of art into just this one kind of fleshless, scaleless Esperanto image? Are we really as completely and passively at the mercy of its legerdemain as he would have us believe? Had Malraux's critics thought to challenge the validity of these assumptions their criticism of the "Museum Without Walls" might have developed into a very constructive and much needed analysis of the actual problems of documenting art photographically; but instead they were provoked by his cavalier attitude toward the integrity of the work of art into making an equally untenable defense of it.

Edgar Wind, for example, makes it clear that he regards the transforming effect of the camera on our vision as nothing less than an aesthetic disaster: "Our eyes have been sharpened to those aspects of painting and sculpture that are brought out by the camera" to the point that "in the artist's own vision we can observe the growth of a pictorial and sculptural imagination that is positively attuned to photography, producing works photogenic to such a degree that they seem to find a vicarious fulfillment in mechanical after-images ... What has optimistically been called the 'museum without walls' is in fact a museum on paper — a paper-world in which the epic oratory of Malraux proclaims, with the voice of a crier in the market place, that all art is composed in a single key, that huge monuments and small coins have the same plastic eloquence if transferred to the scale of the printed page, that a *gouache* can equal a fresco."[3] And Georges Duthuit chose the tenth anniversary of Malraux's book to publish an even more extreme attack, a pamphlet entitled "The Unimaginable Museum" that subsequently he expanded into a three-volume tract.[4] In that work Duthuit argues in effect that there is absolutely no substitute for the physical work of art in its original setting — that the museum embalms it and the photograph distorts it beyond recognition.

Like most cries of heresy these complaints fossilize the very aesthetic reality they mean to defend. For to begin with, the sins of photographic reproductions, whatever else they may be, are far from original. As long ago as 1836, for example, three years before the invention of the daguerreotype, we find Stendhal warning of "the danger of buying *engravings* of fine pictures which one has seen on one's travels. Soon the engraving forms the whole resemblance, and destroys the real memory."[5]But even more to the point, our impressions of paintings are constantly being modified by the impact of *other paintings* more deeply experienced or recently seen. This congress of images is as complex

as it is vital and inevitable, and would exist if no reproductions of any kind had ever been made at all. Nor is the physical work of art still indisputably in situ immune from distortion, or even virtual obliteration by the cacaphony of later accretions. In any case, much of the most important monumental art of Egypt, Assyria and Greece is no longer in situ; we must either form our impressions of it in museums or presumably not at all. Or finally, what about those works that, normally all but inaccessible to the viewer, can be revealed to us by the camera as a privileged observer on the scaffolding or in the restorer's studio? Where, in fact, is the *physical* structure of a medieval window more decipherable, in the cathedrals or in photographs made on the restorer's glazing bench? In short, the more thoroughly one examines the arguments raised by Malraux's critics the less rational — the less relevant to the real problems of art interpretation do they appear to be.

Nor do they reveal any understanding of the way photography actually distorts, impoverishes *or* complements human vision even though it demonstrably does all three. For example, the camera undoubtedly functions as a flagrant de-scaling device, but as the novice photographer soon learns by hard experience, our own vision does something remarkably similar. For whatever fills our attention at any given moment fills it completely, the detail from a Rembrandt etching no less than the Grand Canyon. Indeed, the camera cannot pluck the distant detail out of its context half so readily as the human eye does — a telephoto lens is required — nor can it obliterate the incongruous details of whatever falls within its scope the way our focused vision constantly does. From a purely optical point of view the camera is far more literal than the eye. To be sure, even the best photograph is always bound to be an impoverished duplicate of the work of art, if only because it records but a single isolated moment in the life of that work, as seen from a certain angle and in a certain light, divorced from the many other aspects of it that one can so readily perceive and correlate in the presence of the actual work. Here, surely Malraux's critics have a point, yet even this situation may be turned to one's advantage, as Bernard Berenson realized: "It is a fact, of which long experience alone will fully convince one, that the photograph brings out not only details but aspects of objects that escape our notice. When the work of art is present one cannot avoid enjoying it as a whole and may even identify oneself with it to the point of self-obliteration ... Not so before the photograph, or rather photographs. There, training and habit turn one automatically into the scrutinizing observer and close investigator, who is not easily dazzled by some effect that at the moment appeals irresistibly."[6]

To sum up our conclusions thus far: the camera, far from being either a miracle *or* a monster, is simply an instrument for the recording of certain limited kinds of visual information with great optical precision. As such, its use for good or ill is no more foreordained than that of any other instrument. To say that the photographic representation of the work of art is necessarily pernicious, or invariably inferior to what can be observed in the presence of the work itself is to assume either that the work of art is always ideally accessible or that it may be studied in a neutral context. Both assumptions have been

Right: 119. The *Thaddeus* panel (page 62) during restoration.

Right: 122. Etienne Martin and François Stahly: St-Remy, Baccarat, 1955; and 123. Mark Adams: *Creation* window, St. Andrew's Episcopal Church, Saratoga, California.

shown to be false. Not all works of art are ideally accessible to the viewer; and the notion that they can be studied in a neutral context turns out upon examination to be little more than an abstract ideal, a useful but completely museum-oriented fiction — fine-arts museum with real walls. This was Malraux's valid insight which, alas, he abuses in his "Museum Without Walls"; but it is this insight no less than his abuse of it that his critics seem to have rejected in a kind of Luddite fury, leaving the very real problems involved in visually documenting works of art as unresolved and chaotic as they found them. It is to these problems and this chaos as it may be seen in the existing documentation of stained glass that we shall now turn our attention.

Let us begin with the basic black-and-white archive photographs of the early cathedral windows. In all black-and-white photographs there is the problem of how best to render the spectrum of colors in the subject *tonally* — in shades of gray; how not only to render the dark-and-light values of the various colors individually but in relation to one another. In the case of the early windows this is particularly important because as we have already noted their composition is based to a large extent upon a rich "counterpoint" of ruby and blue figure-and-ground inversions; yet both of these colors are quite saturated and neither is consistently darker or lighter than the other in the windows themselves. Indeed, a given piece of the best handblown glass may contain a considerable range of shading within it, as we have already seen in the *Thadeus* panel

120. and 121. The *Ezekiel* panel (page 78) and its ruby and and blue color "counterpoint."

reproduced on page 62. To render both ruby and blue in approximately the same tonal range is possible, but to do so is to lose all sense of their formal deployment. Therefore, either the one or the other wants to be deliberately darkened or lightened — presumably on the basis of the relative saturation or intensity of the two colors in any given window — and this can be easily enough done with the appropriate combination of film and color filter. Thus one might choose to render the intense blues of the west windows in Chartres a distinct shade lighter than the rubies, while with equal plausibility one might decide to render the more somber blues of the 13th century a shade darker than the ruby; and so on. Admittedly, any such interpretation is bound to be subjective and in the last analysis arbitrary. But here again: just as there is no such thing as a neutral context in which to view the work of art, so there is no such thing as a *technically* neutral photograph. Depending upon how any film is exposed, developed and printed the contrast between darks and lights can be considerably increased or decreased, often to considerable effect as may be seen in the two contemporary works illustrated here. In order to capture the play of light upon the sculptured masonry of the Baccarat window the photographer chose quite properly to minimize contrast; in order to convey some sense of the kinetic color vibration in Mark Adams's *Creation* window the photographer chose to maximize contrast. The choice was absolutely right in both cases, for the particular work in question. In short, the only choice that we have is between a considered and consistent interpretation, which is the least that one might expect from what purports to be the scholarly documentation of an art, and gross unnecessary confusion. This brings us back to the stained-glass windows in the scholars' own "Museum Without Walls."

In Delaporte's comprehensive catalog *Les Vitraux de la cathédrale de Chartres* which was published in 1926,[7] the photographer Etienne Houvet chose to render all the blues — not only the brilliant blues of the 12th century but those of the 13th century as well — as a pure *white,* and all of the rubies as a black or near-black. That is to say, he chose to work for maximum contrast in order to bring out as clearly as possible the linear design and basic color massing of the windows, and in this he succeeded admirably — but at the cost of losing almost all sense of the texture and substance of the glass itself. Crystal clear and sharp as his photographs are, they remind one of nothing so much as a kind of up-dated version of the engravings in "Vitrail" (page 46.) Some twenty years later, when the west windows were photographed again prior to their reinstallation in the cathedral after World War II, essentially the same technique was employed, as may be seen in the *Herod* panel reproduced on page 53. In the blue of Herod's outer garment and in those of the other figures one finds only the most aqueous hint of substance, while the ruby background of the panel is still rendered as an all-but impenetrable black.

At the same time, however, Sidney Pitcher was producing a very different, and to my mind far superior, photographic interpretation of the English windows, as may be seen in Herbert Read's *English Stained Glass.*[8] To compare Houvet's Christ from the Chartres *Jesse Tree* with the Canterbury *Adam* is to realize what the French photographers sacrificed in textural fidelity to the quality of the ancient glass. Instead of working for maximum contrast the Canterbury photographer has concentrated on bringing as much as possible into the middle of the gray scale, and he has rendered the ruby border of the panel a shade lighter than its blue background. In our print of *Lot's Wife*, however, the blue begins to verge on black, while the ruby in the border and burning city are nearly white — almost the exact opposite of the French rendition of these same two colors. How forced *both* extremes are may be judged by referring again to my own photograph of the *Thadeus* panel on page 62, which was made on standard panchromatic film without any filter or special treatment whatsoever.

The problem of color reproduction need not detain us here, because it is both more generally recognized and less distinctively related to stained glass than is the manner in which photographic reproductions, whether in black-and-white or color, are presented on the printed page. For this, far from being the mere matter of book design that it is commonly taken to be, is a matter of the utmost interpretive significance. To put it in a nutshell: *the employment of white margins around any photographic reproduction vastly increases its apparent visual autonomy; "bleeding" the photographic reproduction off the edges of the page vastly reduces its apparent visual autonomy.* That reproductions of easel paintings are normally "framed" with such margins is an especially apt convention, for by this means it is set off from its typographical surroundings in much the same way that the originals are by their own physical frames. The moment that such an image runs to the edge of the page a very different effect is created. We can no longer be sure whether or not it has not been arbitrarily cropped to make *it* fit the page. To be sure, any reproduction may actually be cropped whether printed with margins or not — we are always at the mercy of the photographer and the platemaker; but the crucial point is that margins bestow upon the reproduction a distinct sense of visual autonomy whereas their elimination tends to make it "muralesque with respect to the page."[9]

So deeply ingrained is the convention of employing margins, however, that far more often than not they are employed where they are completely inappropriate, as the illustrations on pages 184 and 185 make clear. Reproduced in what is still the prevalent academic manner, Houvet's details from a window in Chartres are barely distinguishable from ceramic tiles; the overall windows from oriental rugs. By comparison, the completely *glassless* windows on the two succeeding pages clearly evoke far more of the qualities of stained glass as we actually experience it in the presence of the real thing. Obviously, the stained-glass window is bounded and defined less by its own physical edges than by its *aura;* from a strictly luminous or expressive point of view *it has no determinate edges at all.* To pluck it from its luminous environment and reproduce it as though it were a completely static, self-contained pictorial image is therefore far more insidious than anything in the "Museum Without Walls." All the more so, because whereas Malraux's photographic contrivances are generally both dramatic and obvious, and are clearly referred to as "fictitious" by Malraux himself,[10] this academic fiction has by now acquired the protective coloring of a norm.

Page 180: 124. *Christ in Glory*, Jesse Tree window, Chartres Cathedral, c. 1155.

Page 181: 125. *Adam*, Canterbury Cathedral, c. 1200.

And yet one thing must immediately be conceded in its defense: the stained-glass window is often extremely difficult to photograph in its setting without becoming enmeshed in a whole host of interpretive problems for which there are no ready solutions. Consider, for example, the photographs reproduced on pages 188, 189, and 190. In the first one the correct "picture plane" of the window has been preserved but we are given only the most minimal indication of its relation to its setting. In the second, which is an angle shot, this quality is lost but the relation of the window to its surroundings is very effectively conveyed. In the third as in the first photograph the setting of the stained glass is lost in darkness, but here again, because it is an angle shot these windows seem to have a kind of "breathing space" that is altogether lacking in the first photograph. Which then is the more accurate form of representation, that which is planometrically correct or that which is more spatially evocative?

Or again, consider the two very different photographs of the chancel window in St. George's Church, Durham, N.H., on page 191. In the first, which was taken without the aid of any artificial lighting, the window seems to loom out of a cavernous darkness. Though completely uncontrived this photograph nevertheless falsely dramatizes its actual appearance. In the second photograph this pitfall was avoided through the use of floodlights, yet here too the effect seems somehow stagey and unconvincing. Suddenly we realize why: the cast shadows on the chancel wall, especially to the left of the altar, betray the fact that the stained-glass window is not the governing source of light here that it normally is in actuality. This is a purely technical failing and one that the photographer might have avoided; far worse is the bloom of light that he has deliberately created just over the altar. This is pure incandescent corn.

How, then, ought the art of stained glass to be visually documented? It would seem that we are confronted with three rather distinct possibilities. First, we may conclude, with Edgar Wind and Georges Duthuit hovering over our shoulder, that the photographic reproduction is little more than a counterfeit — a necessary evil at best. If we do so it follows as a matter of principle that the serious monograph should be illustrated with the least possible number of deliberately lackluster cuts gathered in a lump at the end of the book, where their distinctive pallor and inconvenience will declare them to be nothing more than visual footnotes to the text. Or second, following Malraux, we may conclude that the photographic reproduction is a full-fledged aesthetic entity in its own right, quite apart from whatever it represents. If we do this we may plausibly claim that the collection of and dissertation upon such reproductions is a perfectly legitimate activity. But we should realize that it is less art history or even art criticism in the strict sense than a kind of visual-verbal collage — a new art form in which the peculiarities of photographic reproductions become a positive element. Or third, we may recognize with Bernard Berenson that even though photography is "an instrument in the hands of the manipulator, and an uncertain instrument at that,"[11] it is nevertheless an instrument whose very shortcomings can sometimes be informative. We will then employ photographic reproductions to tell us whatever they can be

Left: 126. *Lot's Wife*, Canterbury Cathedral, early 13th century.

183

127. and 128. *Life of Joseph* window, Chartres Cathedral, early 13th century; details.

Right: 129 and 130. The *Passion* and *Jesse Tree* windows, Chartres Cathedral, c. 1155.

Page 186: 131. Cloister tracery, Lérida.

Page 187: 132. Bamboo lattice-work window in the Japanese pavilion, Brooklyn Botanical Garden.

Page 188: 133. Ludwig Schaffrath: Church of Sts. Peter and Paul, Heilbronn, 1969.

Page 189: 134. David Wilson: Little Sisters of the Assumption, New York, 1966.

136. and 137. Robert Sowers: St. George's Church, Durham, N.H., 1955.

made to tell us — whether straightforwardly or as a consequence of their distortions or false emphases; whether individually, by juxtaposition, or cumulatively in series — about the nature of the actual physical work or works of art under consideration.

The fact that I have adopted the third approach here should not be allowed to obscure my point, which finally boils down to this: recognition that the deployment of illustrations in an art book, far from being a mere matter of abstract "book design," *is always a visual statement about the nature, meaning and importance of the works being illustrated.* Hence the most modest functional illustrations may be truly informative, as they are in Peter Mollica's excellent *Stained Glass Primer,*[12] or the most beautiful colorplates mindlessly bedazzling when laid on a dozen to a page as they are in Lawrence Lee, George Seddon and Francis Stephens' *Stained Glass.*[13] The chief trouble with the scholarly literature on stained glass is that it tends toward but does not wholeheartedly enough commit itself to the first, or as one is tempted to call it, the "in-group ugly" approach. Ugliness, one may think, is hardly in need of converts; but what is one to make of a book like *Le Vitrail française,* the standard reference on French stained glass?[14] The text, written conjointly by several of the leading authorities on the subject, is richly informative; indeed, many of the essays are models of their kind; but this book, far from being the visual delight that its elaborately embossed cover, fancy endpapers and copious illustrations seem to promise, is a complete visual disaster. Nearly a quarter of its more than two hundred black-and-white reproductions were made from disgracefully poor photographs. In plate after plate the lighter parts of the windows, which is to say most of the significant details, are so over-exposed that they are completely "burnt out" and we are left with nothing but a glaring halatory white.

Left: 135. Wilhelm Buschulte: St. Dionysius, Essen-Borbeck.

Some of the windows are reproduced from crudely aligned paste-ups of unevenly exposed panel-by-panel details; still others are barbarously retouched, grotesquely silhouetted or even, in a few instances, out-of-focus. Three are printed on a matt gray stock and therefore have no more luminosity than a poor newspaper cut. The book's thirty-two colorplates run the gamut from reasonable acceptable to one, a detail of the south transept in Chartres, that is as shockingly off-register as the Sunday comic strips. Its layout is a tawdry affront to the French tradition of distinguished book design. The vast north rose of Notre Dame is reproduced scarcely larger than the palm of one's hand, and nowhere in the book is there a photograph that effectively conveys the relation of such a major ensemble of stained glass to its architectural setting. The chapter on contemporary stained glass contains an embarrassing array of third-rate work and no illustrations at all of Matisse's windows in Vence; the photograph of Léon Zack's window-wall in Notre-Dame-des-Pauvres is pitifully inadequate and that of Léger's windows in Audincourt is silhouetted in an extremely arbitrary and distractive manner. To whom was this book visually addressed? And to what end?

When the pseudo-objectivity of noninterpretation results in this kind of thing the confessed poetic aberrations of Malraux seem positively benign.

XII *The Inadvertent Avant-Gardism of Stained Glass*

As we have seen, the art of stained glass tends to "dissolve" even the most exalted painting in the creation of its most spectacular and indelible effects, much as choral music may swallow up even the most important sacred text. Indeed, the great calligraphic painting in the early medallion windows is so strictly subordinated to the overall effect of these windows that one is almost tempted to call it "an art within an art." At the same time, however, the best stained glass, whether ancient or modern, enters into an indissoluble relationship with its architectural setting, in which each vitally qualifies the form, luminous effect, and overall expressive import of the other. For both reasons — its absorption of painting and its refusal of autonomy — the art of stained glass is bound to frustrate the aesthetic expectations of the viewer whose primary orientation is to the pictorial tradition of European painting from c. 1400 until our own time. Which is to say, the aesthetic expectations of most viewers. Meanwhile, those expectations are still being reinforced by the basic structure of the contemporary art world itself.

Until the recent wave of anti-museum activities the art world had become so highly museum- and gallery-oriented that it could scarcely credit as art anything that was not readily and regularly exhibited within its own special milieu. But not only had the art world become extremely *place*-oriented; it continues to be even more determinedly *occasion*-oriented — circumscribed by its own stream of current events, whether the latest avant-garde development or the latest reassessment of Art Nouveau, Poussin or pre-Columbian pottery. One need not decry this state of affairs to realize that in almost every respect stained glass is an outsider, a mode of expression that is all but exhibition- and event-proof. For stained-glass windows are usually commissioned directly from the artist; normally bought and sold just one time, they also entail the commitment of a particular space to a particular work for an indefinitely long time. This is a phenomenon in which all a priori advocates of the next new thing in art have every reason to remain profoundly uninterested. But had they examined this art form more carefully it might have led them to an even more disconcerting conclusion. For they would have discovered that many of the most studiously cultivated and breathlessly proclaimed innovations in the art of the post-Pop era have always been intrinsic, inescapable, not to say commonplace, elements in stained glass. In this least understood, this most stubbornly archaic mode of expression, extremes meet, familiar categories are confounded and the avant-garde pretensions of much recent art are called into question — which, when one comes to think of it, is no mean avant-garde feat in itself.

Nostalgia for a De-aestheticized Factuality

In Minimal, Process and Conceptual art, and Earthworks there may be sensed a common motivation, an effort to escape the conventional terms of the Art Object as nurtured by the museum-gallery milieu; to somehow get beyond the aesthetic. But this is an impossibility because, as Harold Rosenberg has pointed out, the contemporary aesthetic self-consciousness always manages to keep abreast of such strategems: "Even the most haphazard scattering of debris, if carried out in the milieu of art, has become purposive through the fact that accident is by now a fifty-year-old technique for creating art."[1]

This is a problem that could never have arisen in the case of stained glass. For on the one hand, the structural and functional requirements of the stained-glass window *as* a window have always asserted themselves with an unassailable factuality. Whatever else it may be, the stained-glass window is manifestly a physical object; it does indeed keep out the birds and the rain, as our 7th-century chronicler observed; even *La Belle Verrière* is expected to do as much. Moreover, the picture plane of the stained-glass window proclaims its own literal existence with a tenacity that, as we have already seen, defeated all of the virtuoso illusionist techniques of the 16th and 17th centuries. On the other hand, however, as *La Belle Verrière* also attests, such factuality is by no means incompatible with the most ravishing display of pure aesthetic effects — and this quite outside the museum-gallery world.

Art as the Interaction of the Art Object with its Surroundings

According to Robert Morris, one of the leading Minimal sculptors, "The better new work takes relationships out of the work and makes them a function of space, light, and the viewer's field of vision." Takes them out of the work because — so Morris claims — it is impossible to establish a mutually affective bond between the work and these other elements without reducing the work itself to the simplest geometric form: "Every internal relationship, whether it be set up by a structural division, a rich surface, or what have you, reduces the public, external quality of the object and tends to eliminate the viewer to the degree that these details pull him into an intimate relation with the work and out of the space in which the object exists . . . The sensuous object, resplendent with compressed internal relations, has had to be rejected."[2]

Not in stained glass. As the illustration on page 104 makes clear, the stained-glass artist, far from having to labor in order to establish an interaction between his work and its surroundings, can hardly avoid it.

Deliberate Craftsmanship vs. the Cultivation of Accidental Effects

To quote Harold Rosenberg again, "Art in our era oscillates between the conviction that meeting the resistance of a craft tradition is indispensable to acts of creation and the counter-conviction that secrets can be fished alive out of the sea of phenomena."[3] This is another dilemma that, so far as the art of stained glass is concerned, can hardly be said to exist. For to begin with, the stained-glass artist's commitment to his craft is, and must be, absolute. Natural light, the light-adaptive behavior of the human eye, and the structural properties of glass simply are what they are; they can be effectively manipulated only to the degree that one understands and exploits *their* essential characteristics.

At the same time, however, this commitment to craft does not deny — rather, it presupposes and confidently exploits — a whole retinue of happy accidents, in the texture and shading of the glass, but even more in the constantly changing patterns of light that play upon it, so various that no one can ever foresee them in all of their manifold particularity. Indeed, it is the promise of such happy accidents that, more than anything else, compensates the stained-glass artist for the relative intractibility of his medium. This is also why the interior artificial-light installation of a stained-glass window, which freezes its luminous life into a single, flat, static moment of itself, is a barbarism. In effect, it converts the stained-glass window into a life-size Kodachrome of itself.[4]

Kineticism, Luminism and Programmed Art

Common to these movements is not only a reaction against the "fetishism of the Art Object" but a deliberate turning away from the traditional resources of art to those of technology. Of particular interest to us here are the curiously unsatisfactory results that have been obtained whenever motion, whether of materials or of light, has been created *mechanically*. For example, Naum Gabo, one of the early kineticists, explained in 1937 why he had quit making motorized works: "Mechanics has not yet reached that stage of absolute perfection where it can produce real motion in a sculptural work without killing, through the mechanical parts, the pure sculptural content, because the motion is of importance and not the mechanism that produces it."[5] And after some early experiments with mechanization Alexander Calder also abandoned it in favor of his now-classic mobile sculpture, whose motion is governed solely by the random effects of air currents. More recently Dan Flavin, a leading contemporary light artist, categorically rejected on principle *all* mechanized multi-sensory techniques. In a statement with the savagely comic title, " 'About the Individual Cost of Brave New Worldly Artistic Sensorial Technocracy' or 'Should You Believe: There's No Buzz Like "Strobe" Biz?'," Flavin condemns light shows as "easy, mindless, indiscriminate sensorial abuse to any audience, for vaguely construed notions of attention-getting 'control' . . . psychologically intimidating, even dangerous, to individuals." And speaking of his own work with fluorescent lights, Flavin says, "I aim constantly for clarity and distinction."[6]

Even if one does not fully share Flavin's misgivings, it must be conceded that Willoughby Sharp, one of the chief proponents of kineticism and luminism, does little to dispel them. "A spectacle demands *total* audience involvement," he proclaims, eerily echoing some of the most offensive political rhetoric of our century. "We have reached the end of disinterestedness, impartiality, and contemplation. We are embarking on a new phase of artistic awareness in which interest, partiality, and involvement are the chief characteristics."[7] If this is in fact their intent, the recalcitrant amongst us must wonder whether the saving grace of the most successful luminous and kinetic art has not been its *lack* of total control. Surely, one of the primary attractions of a Calder mobile is the fact that its motion is totally unprogrammed, infinitely variable within the limits established by the various, clearly articulated fulcrums and axes of the particular work. Elegantly, insouciantly, like choreographed smoke curls, it fairly dances on the air.

On the ethics of control, however, the cathedral windows still offer us the most impressive evidence — especially when we try to imagine the world into which they were introduced. For as Aldous Huxley reminds us, the great mass of people in the pre-industrial world were, by modern standards, almost color- and light-starved. They possessed "only homespun and a few vegetable dyes; and, for interior decoration there were at best the earth colors . . . before every pair of eyes was only the dark squalor of the family hovel, the dust or mud of the village street . . . Hence a passionate, an almost desperate thirst for bright, pure colors; and hence the overpowering effect produced by such colors whenever, in church or court, they were displayed . . . The illumination of a city . . . was a rare event, reserved for victories and national holidays, for the canonization of saints and the crowning of kings. Now it occurs nightly and celebrates the virtues of gin, cigarettes and toothpaste."[8] Yet no matter how easily overwhelming the early windows may have been, combined as they were with noble architecture, haunting music, glorious pageantry and religious fervor, they appear never to have lost that final element of reserve, of which we have already spoken. Perhaps this was their ultimate grace: that neither in their color or form, or the urgency of their message, were they tempted to obliterate one's orientation to the sun in its rounds, whose energies could always speak directly to the viewer as they still do in Chartres.

CONCLUSION

The principle that each art should be rooted in its own distinctive resources as a medium is by no means new. First advanced by Aristotle, it was taken up again in the 18th century by the German critic and playwright Gottold Lessing in his influential essay on the *Laocoon*,[1] and further refined by the late-19th-century English philosopher Bernard Bosanquet in his *Three Lectures on Aesthetics.*[2] More recently Henri Focillon in his *Vie des Formes,*[3] and D. W. Gotschalk in *Art and the Social Order,*[4] have emphasized the inherent formal attributes of the materials and techniques employed in the various arts. And yet for most contemporary writers on art the claims of the medium have seemed both too obvious and too limited to merit anything more than the most perfunctory acknowledgment. Thus the sculptor and critic Sidney Geist recently declared that "materials have their sensuous qualities and structural properties, but no intrinsic artistic content, and a mystique of materials is limiting, delusive, and finally a concern of craftsmen. 'Love of material' is a psychological, not a sculptural, affair; 'truth to material' is a truth which changes from style to style and sculptor to sculptor."[5]

One need not quarrel with this statement about wood or stone or bronze to realize how utterly inadequate it becomes when applied to the phenomenon of light. Even if we accept for argument's sake the notion that love of light is nothing more than a "psychological" affair — whether in Stonehenge, amongst the original Platonists or in 12th-century Chartres — the behavior of light is so sovereign and its life-giving energies so manifest that it is only with an effort that one can think of it as a *material* phenomenon at all; nor can we reasonably deny the whole complex array of elemental emotions that light in all of its moods inescapably evokes, nurtures and sustains. They are far too immediate to be denied, however we choose to interpret them. As long as the early glassworkers understood this, however intuitively, they could and did adapt to their own special requirements the skills and techniques of half a dozen widely different arts from painting to metalsmithing without mongrelizing their own. As we have already seen, the art of the great cathedral windows was nothing if not a triumph of assimilation. But once attention became focused upon its representational function no amount of technical innovation or refinement could save it. Rather, each new skill tended to be developed hypertrophically for its own sake, thus if anything actually hastening the decline of the art. To ignore the most sensuous, immediate and dynamic effects of light was eventually to become bedazzled by them because, to say it once more, they are inescapably there, chaotically disordered when not positively and intelligibly ordered.

Thus critics, and historians too, lacking any comprehension of the manner in which the stained-glass window and its setting each modifies the effect of the other, would come to ignore this phenomenon altogether (as did Berenson); or would attribute to early glass painting qualities that it neither sought, required, nor could have produced (as did Viollet-le-Duc). Or, in an effort to somehow account for the uncomprehended splendors of the great cathedral windows would invoke (as countless writers have done) the "spirit of the age" — as if communal enthusiasm however exalted could ever have been responsible for the complex adjustments of stained glass to architecture and architecture to stained glass, tentatively, cumulatively, by trial-and-error, at numerous sites, over who knows how long a time. And rare is the critic who would have the self-perception let alone the grace to concede with Malraux that "even today we hardly understand the language of the stained-glass window."

Here, in sum, is an art form whose most vital element is a natural force; an art that utterly refuses to be reduced to a congeries of mere dumb stuff upon which the artist imposes order and significance by a completely independent act of will. It is an art that calls for the same kind of empathetic engagement — the same "mixture of cunning, boldness and humility," to borrow a phrase from Sybil Moholy-Nagy[6] — that the creators of anonymous architecture have always addressed to such implacable realities as climate, terrain, the durability and aging characteristics of their materials. I realize that to speak of humility even in the same breath with boldness and cunning is to run the risk of misunderstanding. The romanticist that is in all of us detects a hidden threat to the free play of the imagination, while the technocrat that is his alter ego bridles at the notion that there could be any physical phenomenon that cannot be bent to one's will by an exercise of sufficient mechanical ingenuity. Let me therefore try to make my point in another way. It is nothing more nor less than a call for direct, unmediated receptivity to the singular strengths and limitations of *this* mode of expression, viewed as an end in itself rather than as a surrogate for any other. Viewed as I assume it must have been viewed in the age of its greatest achievement. If it had not been so notoriously *mis*interpreted, if it had not become the victim of so many Procrustean *mis*conceptions, I should not have had to write this book.

So thoroughly has Western art been shaped by the canons of autonomous easel painting that until very recently no other medium seemed quite real until our experience of it was verified in this one princely medium. Thus the art historian Millard Meiss informs us that Jan Van Eyck's painting of the *Virgin in the Church* is "the earliest document we possess, apart from the buildings themselves, of the actual appearance of the interior of a Gothic cathedral." And he continues: "Not until two hundred years after the construction of the churches themselves was a painter able to capture the qualities of space and light of their interiors. But if the artists of his time in the Low Countries enjoyed debating the relative merits of the several arts, as they did in Italy, we can surmise Jan's contribution to the 'paragone.' He would have argued of course for the supremacy of painting, and his thesis might conceivably have been that painting is not only the one art which can truly mirror the world, but that it incorporates, in a sense, the other arts. As proof he could point to the church, the sculpture, and the beautiful specimen of goldsmith's work in the *Virgin in the Church.*"[7] Thus venturing to speak for Van Eyck does Professor Meiss echo the imperiously reductive claims made for easel painting half a millenium ago — painting as a veritable "Museum Without Walls" some four hundred years before the invention of photography. Thus does he portray this supposed feat as an unalloyed triumph of art — as if *any* image however fine could possibly duplicate the experience of being in any great building; and this at the very moment when the ability to create an actual cathedral was ceasing to exist.

At the same time, however, one can detect stirrings in the opposite direction. In a recent essay on Matisse's painting *La Conversation* Pierre Schneider declares that "the freeing of drawing and color from the duty of representation, of limitation imposed by the styles of perspective, by the illusionist fiction that had governed the art of painting since the Renaissance, delivered painting from its model, from chiaroscuro. No longer having to submit to degradation, color and drawing were restored to what in the chemical sense can be called their essence: pure tone and line." This much we have heard before, but Schneider goes on to invest it with a new significance: "Now these are the very characteristics of great religious art, whether of Romanesque Europe, Byzantium or Islam. How could the similarity, indeed the identity of formal means not lead us to infer a resemblance at the level of the spirit?" And he concludes that "the old 'what,' the representation that was the principal task of Western art for nearly five centuries, is an obstacle to this manifestation of spirituality, a veil interposed between our eyes and the new sun of the soul . . .

"The universe, mastered and miniaturized thanks to the laws of perspective, becomes an *objet d'art,* a collector's item. Completely different is the image of painting which Matisse's window [in *La Conversation*] is the bearer . . . it is enthroned: frontal, two-dimensional, radiant, expanding. Not a reflection but the source of light. Not hollowing out a fictive space beyond its surface, but projected, beginning with the picture plane, toward us. Shaped for real space, which is the place, common to everyone, where communication and communion are established."[8]

The history of art, like the history of anything else, abounds in majestic ironies. In its own way and pursuing its own ends, the art world, without quite realizing it, would seem to be rediscovering the aesthetic principles that eight centuries ago found their most magnificent expression in the art of stained glass.

NOTES

Introduction
1 *An Aesthetic Approach to Byzantine Art,* London, 1955, p. 171.

I *Discovering What Was "Lost"*
1 Significantly, there is no general treatise on the aesthetics of light; only one that deals thoroughly with light in painting: Wolfgang Schöne, *Ueber das Licht in der Malerei,* Berlin, 1954. Perhaps the tentative formulations in this book will serve as the goad and stimulus for such a study.
2 *Aesthetics and History,* Garden City, N.Y., 1948; Anchor Books ed., New York, 1954, pp. 87-88.
3 *The Voices of Silence,* New York, 1953, p. 38.
4 *New York Times,* December 26, 1971.
5 *The Radiance of Chartres,* New York, 1965, p. 14.
6 "The Eye of Ra," *Light in Art,* Thomas B. Hess and John Ashbury, eds., New York, 1969, pp. 21-36.
7 See, for example, John Piper, "Art or Anti-Art," *Architectural Stained Glass,* Brian Clarke, ed., New York, 1979.

II *The Signal Ambience*
1 Kenneth Clark, *Ruskin Today,* London, 1964; Peregrine Books edition, 1967, p. 178.

III *Inside Light vs. Outside Light*
1 See James R. Johnson, *The Radiance of Chartres, Chapter I, op. cit.,* for an especially interesting discussion of this phenomenon.
2 Evan Hadingham, *Circles and Standing Stones,* New York, 1976, p. 106.

IV *Metamorphosis of the Window*
1 John Knowles, "Leaded Lights and Ornamental Glazing," *Jour. of the Br. Soc. of Master Glass-Painters,* VII, 3, 1938, p. 134.
2 Otto von Simson, *The Gothic Cathedral,* New York, 1956; Bollingen paperback ed., Princeton, 1964, p. 4.
3 *Ibid.,* p. 122.
4 Except for the Cistercians, who in the 12th century insisted on clear glass and with its glare doubtless achieved the requisite degree of Puritanical astringency.

V *Radiance*
1 *Medieval Stained Glass, A Translation of the Article Vitrail,* Francis P. Smith, Atlanta, 1946. All subsequent quotations from "Vitrail" are from Smith's translation.
2 *Ibid.,* p. 18.
3 Johnson, op. cit., p. 42.
4 *Ibid.,* p. 43; Johnson's italics.
5 *Natural-Light Photography,* New York, 1952, p. 6.
6 However true this may be, it cannot be taken as an excuse for the techniques employed in the recent controversial restoration of these windows. At issue here is not merely the loss of a familiar if somewhat over-romanticized image, as claimed by the restorers, but the wholesale employment of irreversible techniques on the single most important ensemble of medieval stained glass extant. The original appearance of these windows is one thing; the effect of a plastic coating on the refractory qualities of ancient glass is another; the long-term physical effects of that coating still another. To argue, as one apologist for the restorers has, that it was necessary to "destroy"

the familiar Chartres blue in order to "save" the west windows is to adopt for restoration work the crazed logic of Viet Nam. For a more detailed analysis of the appearance of the windows prior to their restoration, see Robert Sowers, "On the Blues in Chartres," *Art Bulletin,* XVIII, 2, 1966.

7 *Color Order and Harmony,* New York, 1964, p. 44.

8 Rudolf Arnheim and Eduard F. Sekler, review of Otto Schubert, *Optik in Architektur und Städtbau, Jour. of the Soc. of Arch. Historians,* XXVIII, 1, 1969, p. 78: "Maertens established the angle chosen by the average observer to see a painting on the wall comfortably as 27°, corresponding to a distance about double the length of the picture's longer dimension." Since the individual narrative panels in the *Life of Christ* window are only about forty inches square, the optimum distance for viewing them as paintings would be just under seven feet. In fact they must normally be viewed from roughly *ten times* that distance. For a further discussion of the 13th-century re-use of the west windows in the present cathedral see Robert Sowers, "The 12th-Century Windows in Chartres: Some Wayward Lessons from the 'Poor Man's Bible,'" *Art Journal,* XVIII, Winter 1968-69.

VII *The Fabric of a Stained-Glass Window*

1 For a 12th-century account, see Theophilus (Rugerus), *Diversarum Artium Schedula,* translated by Robert Henrie, London, 1847; Chicago, 1963; also, Mojair S. Frinta, "A Note on Theophilus, Maker of many Wonderful Things," *Art Bulletin,* XLVI, December 1964. pp. 525-29.

2 Viollet-le-Duc, *op. cit.,* p. 23.

VIII *Luminous Reality vs. Pictorial Illusion*

1 *New York Times, op. cit.*

2 *The Dynamics of Architectural Form,* Berkeley, 1977, p. 171.

3 See Arthur Lane, "Florentine Painted Glass and the Practice of Design," *Burlington Magazine,* February 1949, p. 551.

4 *The Architecture of Humanism,* London, 1914; Anchor Books ed., New York, 1954, pp. 89-90 and 34.

5 *Ibid.,* p. 55.

6 *Ibid.,* p. 58.

7 *Ibid.,* pp. 71-72; Scott's italics.

8 *Ibid.,* pp. 61, 64.

IX *The Revival of Stained Glass*

1 *Hints on Glass Painting,* Oxford, 1847; still remarkably readable and informative.

2 A. Charles Sewter, *The Stained Glass of William Morris and His Circle,* New Haven, two volumes, 1974, 1975.

3 *English Stained Glass,* London, 1926, pp. 222-24.

4 *Ibid.,* pp. 225-26.

5 Carlton Lake, "Marc Chagall: Artist at Work," *Atlantic,* July 1963.

6 *New York Times,* September 19, 1964.

7 Konrad Pfaff, *Ludwig Schaffrath, Stained Glass + Mosaic,* Krefeld and C & R Loo, Emeryville, Cal., 1978. See also Robert Kehlmann, "Schaffrath: Stained Glass + Mosaic," *Craft Horizons,* March-April 1978, and Ed Carpenter, "Windows, walls: structural dialogue between equals," *Smithsonian,* February 1978.

8 Paul Wember, *Johan Thorn Prikker,* Krefeld, 1966; and August Hoff, *Johan Thorn Prikker,* Recklinghausen, 1958.

X *The Quest for Autonomy*

1 See Robert Sowers, "Autonomy as a Spurious Absolute," *Architectural Stained Glass,* Brian Clarke, ed., *op. cit.*

2 Robert Kehlmann, "Books," *Craft Horizons,* February 1977, pp. 18f.

3 *Glass Art,* January-February 1973, p. 18.

4 New York, January 26-March 17, 1978.

5 "Lead and Glass Drawings," *Stained Glass,* Fall 1978, p. 181.

6 See, for numerous examples, Otto B. Rigan, *New Glass,* San Francisco, 1976; and Narcissus Quagliata, *Stained Glass from Mind to Light,* San Francisco, 1976.

XI *Stained-Glass Windows in the "Museum Without Walls"*

1 This is the title of Volume I of *The Psychology of Art,* and Part I of *The Voices of Silence,* the revised one-volume version of the *Psychology,* published in New York in 1953. It is from the latter that I quote.

2 *Ibid.,* 13-14, 44 and 46.
3 *Art and Anarchy,* London, 1963, pp. 76-77.
4 See Andre Chastel, "The Revolt Against Malraux," *New York Times,* May 26, 1957.
5 *The Life of Henry Brulard,* New York, 1925, p. 334; my italics.
6 *Aesthetics and History, op. cit.,* p. 224.
7 Chartres, four volumes.
8 London, 1926.
9 Sidney Tillem, "Walker Evans: Photography as Representation," *Artforum,* March 1967, p. 18. So little is the framing function of margins understood that in her recent tract *On Photography* (New York, 1977, p. 128) Susan Sontag treats them as a pure status symbol: photographers who insist on their works being reproduced with margins are simply "invoking a model inherited from another art: as paintings are put in frames, photographs should be framed in white space."
10 Malraux, *op. cit.,* p. 24.
11 *Aesthetics and History, op. cit.,* p. 223.
12 Berkeley, Volume I, 1971; Volume II, 1977.
13 London and New York, 1976.
14 Paris, 1956; Marcel Aubert, Andre Chastel, et al.

XII *The Inadvertent Avant-Gardism of Stained Glass*
1 *The De-definition of Art,* New York, 1972; Collier Books edition, 1973, p. 68.
2 "Notes on Sculpture," Part II, *Artforum,* October 1966, p. 23. For a strenuous objection to the Minimalist conception of art espoused by Morris see Michael Fried, "Art and Objecthood," *Artforum,* Summer 1967.
3 Rosenberg, *op. cit.,* pp. 37-38.
4 Not too long after this was written I was presented with the problem of an existing building whose two huge balcony windows were hopelessly boxed in by buildings on either side. It was a case of using artificial light or not having stained glass at all, in a space that clearly stood to benefit by the color and design, if not the full range of effects of which this art is capable. I explained my misgivings and made the windows, but still stand behind my statement as a general rule.
5 As quoted by Willoughby Sharp in "Luminism and Kineticism," *Minimal Art,* Gregory Battcock, ed., New York, 1968, pp. 351-52.
6 "Some Other Comments," *Artforum,* December 1967, pp. 20-21. See also, "Lights! Lights!," Harold Rosenberg, *Artworks and Packages,* New York, 1969.
7 Sharp, *op. cit.,* p. 21; my italics.
8 *The Doors of Perception* and *Heaven and Hell,* New York, 1954, Colophon edition, 1963, pp. 114-15.

CONCLUSION

1 First published in 1766; English translation by Ellen Frothingham, London, 1890; New York, 1957.
2 London, 1915.
3 First published in 1934; English translation by Charles B. Hogan and George Kubler, *The Life of Forms in Art,* New York, 1962.
4 First published in 1947; revised edition, New York, 1962.
5 *Brancusi,* New York, 1968, p. 158.
6 *Native Genius in Anonymous Architecture,* New York, 1957, p. 52.
7 "Light as Form and Symbol in Some Fifteenth-Century Paintings," *Renaissance Art,* Creighton Gilbert, ed., New York, 1970, p. 68.
8 "The Striped Pajama Icon," *Art in America,* July-August 1975, pp. 78 and 82.

PHOTOGRAPHIC CREDITS

All diagrams and most photographs not otherwise credited are by the author.
Ashmolean Museum, 17.
Marni Bakst, 111.
Jean Barillet, V.
Inge Bartholemé, 2, 38, 40, I, 65, 67, 86, 97, 101-105, 133.
British Crown Copyright, 8, 9, 44, 49, 58, 121.
British Museum, 50.
Peter Broomell/David Sharpe, 110.
Ed Carpenter, 107.
Desgodetz, 10.
Paul Facchetti, 122.
Fototeca Unione, Roma, 11.
Charles Frizzell, 113.
Hessisches Landesmuseum, Darmstadt, 54, 55, IV.
Etienne Houvet, 124, 127, 128.
Istituto Archeologico Germanico, Roma, 12.
Ray King, 106.
Kingsley, Julia Wirick, 108.
Ned Martin, III, 123.
Joseph W. Molitor, 137.
Anne Münchow, 77.
National Monuments Record, London, 33, 47, 56.
Dr. H. Oidtmann, 27, 39, 76, 78-80, 82-85, 88, 99, 100, 135.
Sidney Pitcher, 46.
H. Roger-Viollet, 24.
Richard Sargent, 117.
Manfred Schäfer, 68, 87, 95, 96.
Edith Schreiter-Diedrichs, 89-94.
Stiftsbibliothek, St. Gall, 16.
David Wilson, 36, 37.
Foto-Zwicker, 69.

INDEX